Sideways To The Top

Sideways To The Top

10 Stories Of Successful Women That Will Change Your Thinking About Careers Forever

Norah Breekveldt

with contributions by
*Dr Hannah Piterman, Dr Kerry Baxter,
Heather Carmody & Hugh Davies*

M

MELBOURNE BOOKS

Published by Melbourne Books
Level 9, 100 Collins Street,
Melbourne, VIC 3000
Australia
www.melbournebooks.com.au
info@melbournebooks.com.au

National Library of Australia
Cataloguing-in-Publication entry

Author: Breekveldt, Norah.
Title: Sideways To The Top : 10 stories of successful
women that will change your thinking about careers
forever.
ISBN: 9781922129178 (paperback)
Subjects: Successful people--Case studies.
Businesswomen--Case studies.
Women--Case studies.
Success--Case studies.
Dewey Number: 158.1

Photos page 8 and 264 © Chery Lyn
Book Design: Ellen Cheng, Melbourne Books

Printed in China

Another Macfarlan Lane Professional Initiative
www.macfarlanlane.com.au

MACFARLAN LANE
Fresh Career Thinking

'Two roads diverged in a wood, and I,
I took the one less traveled by,
And that has made all the difference.'

— Robert Frost

Contents

REFLECTIONS AND CONCLUSIONS

Norah Breekveldt

Norah Breekveldt has over 25 years' line and consulting experience in human resources, change management and organisational effectiveness across a broad range of sectors including government, oil and chemical industry, manufacturing, supply chain distribution and financial services.

She has coordinated the delivery of career transition services internally during her corporate HR roles with top companies and has been directly involved in the provision of career transition services for senior executives and CEOs as a career transition coach since 2007.

Norah has also held a number of directorships on boards of not-for-profit organisations. She is a member of the Australian Institute of Management, a graduate of the Institute of Company Directors (GAICD) and an associate certified coach (ACC) with the International Coaching Federation.

She is a recipient of the Telstra Business Women's Award.

Introduction

This is a book of career stories experienced by successful and high achieving women. Their stories are illustrative of non-linear and unpredictable pathways to career success, where women have effectively challenged the status quo and sidestepped more traditional career-advancement models. All these women recognised opportunities and possessed the courage to take these opportunities to move across geographic locations, industries or disciplines to get to the top. Without exception, these women moved sideways in order to move upwards. Few, if any, have reached their final career destination.

This is also a book of conversations that challenge conventional thinking about how to break through the 'glass ceiling'. These stories and conversations generate fresh career thinking about what career success means for women and how it can be achieved.

The book explores significant turning points that affected these women's lives and shaped their success. It also provides lessons and advice from the women interviewed, as well as insights gleaned from conversations with thought leaders and researchers who have expert knowledge in career transitions, successes and gender differences.

Themes explored in this book include:

- An overview of how each woman built her career and pivotal influences.

- Momentous decisions, big shifts and tough challenges that defined or changed the course of a career.

- Time in the wilderness. What happened in the dark moments?

- Exploring the mentors, guides and trusted advisors along the way.

- Lessons learned and advice and insights for other women.

Why this book and why now?

> *'I don't think that in my lifetime there will be a woman prime minister.'*
> — *Margaret Thatcher,*
>   *Prime Minister of Great Britain (1979–1990), 1971*

The world changes in leaps and bounds, and often in unpredictable ways. Indeed, the world of work has changed significantly for women since Margaret Thatcher shared her opinions in the early 1970s. More flexible employment practices exist and women are increasingly becoming the norm in a growing range of professions and industries. Yet the representation of women in positions of power remains abysmally low. Although women graduates have outnumbered men since the 1980s, a scant six percent of line management positions are held by women and less than four percent of board directorships are held by women (further statistical evidence can be read in the chapters by Dr Hannah Piterman and Catherine Nance).

Many companies have tried multiple initiatives to increase the number of women in their senior ranks or on boards, with limited or no success. Corporate obstacles, unconscious (and conscious) bias and stereotyping may partly explain this lack of progress.

In this context, it would be easy for women to lose heart. It is therefore important to understand that there are paths to career success that have been boldly navigated by women. The conversations in this book show how 11 women have overcome these and other obstacles and taken unconventional career paths to success. All these women come from diverse backgrounds, with very different experiences. There are contradictions and paradoxes across stories. These stories are supplemented by strong research and rigorous debate around contemporary issues and possible ways forward.

Potential ingredients for success

Some of the views expressed throughout the book were provocative, and career success is explained across a range of different and sometimes opposed dimensions. We would be doing the book an injustice, therefore, to generalise about the ingredients for success particularly based on a small number of anecdotal stories. However, we can reflect on several themes that emerged across the stories of these exceptional, successful women. For instance:

- They all embraced the concept of a less-prescribed career path and were open to choosing paths different from the conventional corporate career ladder that may have been on offer. Many chose sideways moves rather than seeking upwards promotion, and this may have contributed to them ultimately becoming more well-rounded senior leaders. Many were prepared to leave when their organisation did not value their contribution. None of them were complacent, or expected the organisation to take care of their careers.

- Some of the women had not directly or personally experienced the glass ceiling (although they acknowledged that they had observed it and it was pervasive in many workplaces) or, if they did, they recognised the signs and left. Several women utilised their gender as a strength that enhanced their career, rather than perceiving it as a barrier.

- Most did not plan their careers or have a firm career destination in mind, but recognised when it was time for them to move and seized opportunities as these arose. They were highly adaptable and made bold career decisions when the time was right. There was no sense that any of these women saw barriers — rather, they saw opportunities.

- Many women came from a background of very strong and supportive parents who instilled in them a strong self-belief in their capability and potential — at home, there were no restrictions placed on them because of their gender. Several had very supportive fathers and others had entrepreneurial parents. This family environment seemed to influence the way they thought about careers and formed their convictions that there were no barriers to success.

- Several had husbands or life partners who relinquished their own careers or changed their jobs so they could support them.

- Many of them were strong and resilient women who worked out how to challenge and influence authority, and how to persuade and advocate for their ideas, even when those around them held a different point of view.

- They were all extremely passionate about what they pursued. They may have worked hard and long, but they all possessed a strong drive for success, coupled with enormous energy and enthusiasm.

- Although many of them talked about the difficulty in managing their work and non-work lives, very few got to a stage of becoming burnt out or stressed — although all of them had had difficult times in their careers.

- They were highly self-aware, understanding and generally open to discussing their personal strengths and shortcomings, and how they leverage these strengths and work around their shortcomings.

Many shades of grey

We expected these stories to reinforce the barriers and limitations on women's careers often discussed in contemporary debates. Some stories definitely exposed these limitations. Yet we also discovered that a number of stories challenged general suppositions or assumptions about barriers to women that seem to have become undisputed truths in some circles. Some of these assumptions include:

- *Women lead differently to men.* The assumption is that they are less hierarchical, display a cooperative and collaborative leadership style and are more concerned for the welfare of others. Some women definitely displayed these traits. However, others also applied leadership traits more often associated with male leadership styles, including a high level of self-confidence and competitiveness, using assertive or even aggressive language and strategies to get the results they wanted, having a high task focus and being highly controlling, and showing a high degree of independence and daring. One woman believed for some time that she needed to 'behave like a man' to be successful, then realised that being true to herself was the key. In other women, these characteristics seemed to be simply a description of their authentic personality traits. Several women had no hesitation in asking for what they wanted, whether it was a pay rise or putting their hand up for a promotion.

- *Successful women are able to balance their work and personal lives.* Many women tell of their struggle with balancing work and family life. All of them worked extremely long hours and many spoke about the need to negotiate family roles and responsibilities with their partners. Several women did not believe work–life balance was achievable while they were building their careers. They acknowledged the hardships of making it to senior leadership positions and the toll it takes on family life.

- *Gender constrains a woman's career.* There was general agreement that women often face more barriers to becoming leaders than men in the corporate world, and that discrimination, bias and stereotyping holds back many women from realising their potential. Yet in some cases women discussed the advantages of being female and the opportunities their gender presented to them, especially in pursuing self-employment.

- *Access to strong mentors or sponsors is critical to breaking through the glass ceiling.* Many of the women were at an age when formal mentoring or sponsorship programs were nonexistent in the early stages of their careers. They succeeded through a complex balance of strong self-belief, self-awareness around their strengths and weaknesses, the use of their own external networks, and their ability to identify and seize opportunities, rather than relying on formal mentoring programs. Several women chose their own mentors — often men in powerful positions. So, sourcing good mentors was important to many, but these were not necessarily sourced through formal mentoring or sponsorship programs.

- *Women support each other through the women's network.*
  A strong network is critical for anyone developing their career, and there were some fantastic examples of women encouraging and sponsoring other women. However, we also observed many instances where women succeeded without using a vast women's network.

More than conjecture — women as successful leaders

In 2012, Australia's first female prime minister, Julia Gillard, made her now-famous 'misogyny speech', in which she quotes Tony Abbott opining: 'What if men are, by physiology and temperament, more adapted to exercise authority or to issue commands [than women]?'

Are women really up to the challenge of leadership? And if so, why do women continue to be underrepresented in senior levels? The stories in this book demonstrate that, despite a range of obstacles, including unconscious bias and stereotyping, women certainly are up to the challenge!

Let's look at some of the research around unconscious biases that continue to disadvantage women. A meta-analysis of the employment prospects of fictitious job applicants shows that, overall, men are rated more favourably than identically experienced women for 'male' jobs. In one 2009 study,[1] over 100 university psychologists were asked to rate the CVs of Dr Karen Miller or

Dr Brian Miller, fictitious applicants for an academic tenure-track job. The CVs were identical, apart from the name. Yet, strangely, the male Dr Miller was perceived (by both male and female reviewers) to have better research, teaching and service experience than the female Dr Miller. Overall, about three-quarters of the psychologists thought Dr Brian was hireable, while under half had the same confidence in Dr Karen.

Also, in 2007, Stanford University professor Shelley Correll and others[2] found that when applicants were evaluated for a job, the assessors viewed what it takes to be successful differently depending on whether the applicant was male or female. For instance, toughness was considered more important than social skills when they evaluated male applicants, and vice versa for female applicants. They also found that stereotyping may be particularly strong against mothers. In their study of applications for a position as head of a marketing department, applicants who identified themselves as mothers were rated about 10 percent less competent, 15 percent less committed to the workplace, and worthy of $11,000 less salary than women applicants who were non-mothers. Yet parenthood served as no disadvantage at all to men.

A stereotype threat is that of being judged or treated poorly in settings where a negative stereotype about your group applies. Take, for example, the stereotypical belief that women are inferior to men in mathematical ability. A study by Catherine Good and others[3] found that, if women and men were asked to complete a maths test on the understanding that it would measure their maths ability, women performed more poorly than men, reinforcing the gender stereotype that women performed more poorly than men in maths. However, when women and men were told prior to completing the test that the tests were equally hard for both sexes, women actually outperformed men, and their maths potential was unleashed. In other words, the way a task is framed can significantly change the outcome.

The lack of role models at the top is also a factor that creates a barrier to women reaching the top. Remaining with maths as our example for the moment, the presence of a woman who excels in maths serves to alleviate that particular stereotype threat. However, the problem of few female role models at the top is far deeper than not being good at maths. As women become increasingly outnumbered by men, they will progressively lose one very effective protection against stereotyping: safety in numbers, with other women as role models they can aspire to. In these circumstances, they can lose their sense of belonging.

So can women truly succeed in male-dominated environments given the obstacles of stereotyping, unconscious bias and their minority status at the top?

Two recent studies have demonstrated that many women have impressive leadership skills. In a recent study by Zenger Folkman[4] of over 7000 leaders, women were rated higher than the men for every leadership competency except one, and scored significantly higher on 12 of these factors. Interestingly, the higher the level of the leaders, the wider that gap grows in favour of women.

Stereotypically female 'nurturing' competencies such as *building relationships, promoting and engaging in self-development or professional development* and *exhibiting integrity* were, unsurprisingly, scored more highly for the women than the men, thereby supporting the stereotype. But, interestingly, the women also scored higher in two stereotypically male traits: *taking initiative* and *driving for results.*

Finally, in a recent study by Accenture[5] of over 500 senior executives from medium to large companies around the world, leaders viewed women as being slightly more resilient than men, indicating a likelihood of choosing or retaining a female over a male if all other things were equal.

Final comments

The women profiled in this book are 'out-of-the-box' women. They break the rules and break the stereotypes, and perhaps this partly explains the complexities, contradictions and paradoxes across their experiences. While they are successful women leaders, many of them had to work harder than men to prove themselves when working in a male-dominated business environment. Yet the strategies they employed and lessons they learned could equally apply to men.

It has not been the intention of this book to provide a formula for success or propose policy frameworks or strategies for corporations. We do not refute the advantages of corporations formalising networking, mentoring or sponsoring programs, and leadership-development programs designed specifically for women or other affirmative-action, diversity and inclusion initiatives. All these programs, when well designed and supported, and introduced in a culture that embraces diversity, can be highly effective.

The business case for achieving gender balance has been well documented elsewhere,[6] and there is a growing body of organisations taking a fresh approach to gender diversity that appear to be making great headway into increasing diversity at all levels. These individual stories enable us to draw individual conclusions.

Progress will be made when organisations move beyond merely 'accommodating' diversity in teams, to assimilating diverse thinking in everything they and their people do. This requires openness in leaders to continually confront their own biases, to challenge and test their organisation's assumptions, and to actively seek out different views.

How to read this book

This book is divided into three sections. The first section provides historical context and concludes with some of the latest research into women's careers today. The second section includes 10 career stories of inspirational women who have succeeded and are still pursuing career success. The final section features discussions on the realities and current issues facing women, through conversations with experts in career transitions and gender differences. The book concludes with a practical checklist and action plan to help women navigate their careers and achieve career success.

By all means, read the book from cover to cover if you wish. However, you may prefer to read the chapters in any order based on your interests, passions and needs. For instance, you may be interested in starting with the research and economic arguments for diversity; you may be fascinated with the future of work, or have a deep curiosity about particular issues, or simply enjoy reading the individual stories. You may be considering a career move, so may want to go straight to the practical checklist for successful careers. You might want to explore how one multinational company is tackling diversity from a culture-change perspective. This book is designed to be flexible in accommodating a range of styles and preferences, so move backwards and forwards as you wish.

Acknowledgments

The stories and research for this book span many different organisations, industries and individuals, and I am very grateful for the feedback, encouragement and active support I received from all the women and men with whom I discussed the book. The process of writing this book demonstrated to me the power of the women's network and the overwhelming generosity of women prepared to tell their stories and to help other women achieve their career dreams.

My warmest thanks go to Heather Carmody for her sound advice about the book's theme, structure and possible contributors and for her exuberant commitment to this book from the beginning, when it was just a vague concept in our minds. Also Emma Russell for her intelligent editing, Christine Sather (Melbourne Marketing Group), Jerril Rechter (VicHealth), Nareen Young and Jane O'Leary (Diversity Council of Australia), Janet Morrison (the Sex Discrimination Commissioner's office), Peter Singer (Consultant), Sean Spence (Sean Spence & Associates) and Hayden Fricke (PeopleScape) for their wise counsel and for introducing me to their network of professional colleagues. I am also indebted to Catherine Fox for her support, practical advice and wisdom, as she opened doors for me and mentored me through the various stages of the book.

My thanks go to Hugh Davies, Macfarlan Lane's Managing Director, who played an essential role in developing the book's concept from the beginning, supported the writing of chapters, and provided the resources to ensure the book was completed. I would also like to thank Susan Moir and Matt Gaffney, Directors at Macfarlan Lane, for their awesome support.

Finally, my thanks go to all the women leaders, and one male leader, who gave generously of their time to be interviewed, who willingly answered many questions about their lives without holding back, and who patiently waited for the book to be published. A special thanks to Dr Hannah Piterman, Dr Kerry Baxter and Heather Carmody, who produced their own chapters — their contributions shared the load and added depth and colour to the book.

CONTEMPORARY RESEARCH FINDINGS

Dr Hannah Piterman

Contemplations on a 30-year Journey

Dr Hannah Piterman is an adviser and coach to senior management and boards in the areas of board performance, leadership development, and gender diversity to an eclectic client base in the public, private and not-for-profit sectors. Hannah publishes in the areas of governance, leadership and diversity, and contributes to public debate in academic journals, the print media and as a presenter at business forums in Australia and internationally. She maintains academic links through her appointment as an Adjunct Associate Professor at Monash University, Melbourne. She is a co-founder of Gender Worx. She is also a member of advisory committees of not-for-profit organisations including the Committee for Economic Development of Australia (CEDA)'s Victoria/Tasmania State Advisory Council.

Hannah is a strong advocate for gender diversity and the benefits that flow from its achievement. Her commitment led her to conduct the acclaimed two-year research sponsored by big business, government and academic organisations, culminating in her book *Unlocking Gender Potential: A Leader's Handbook*, launched by CEDA in 2010.

'The stories we tell are not always the stories we live'

'The task of women's liberation is never finished, because as old structures change, new ones emerge to be transcended — and that task requires the engagement and cooperation of women and men.' [1]

In his book *The Hollow Tree*,[2] Jacob Rosenberg, author and poet, makes the following comment: 'The stories we tell are not always the stories we live.'

Bill George et al.[3] suggest that the journey to authentic leadership begins with understanding one's own story, one's personal narrative. Telling stories about themselves has not always been easy for women. For senior women, in particular, there is the private narrative, the one shared with friends and family, if at all — trials and tribulations, frustrations as well as successes. And there is the public narrative of how women present themselves in the external world. Women are forever navigating this tension, how to be authentic while managing how much of themselves to expose, and getting it right: 'Who is the real Julia?'

Women are vulnerable. Successful women can be idealised as 'extraordinary' women, the superwomen who seamlessly traverse multiple terrains. The more they are idealised, the more they are vulnerable and the more protective they choose to be. Not surprisingly, the stories they convey are ones that are often patterned on the way men tell stories — about success, about an uninterrupted career path and an upward trajectory as work takes centrestage and family is managed without a hiccup.

The real stories are not stories of perfection, of individualism and of seamless career paths. Rather, they are the stories of women juggling family and work, and struggling to meet personal needs for health, for hair and for heart — the things we must do for ourselves so we can do everything else.

The good news is that women are beginning to tell stories in a way they were unable to 10 or even five years ago. The shift is a sign of the times of a new female identity. I recently attended an event where Gail Kelly, CEO of Westpac and eighth most powerful woman in the world according to *Forbes* magazine, relayed her story of going to a job interview for a senior HR role, with two of her four children in tow. Therese Rein, Christine Nixon and many more women are telling stories that convey a journey of who they are and what they stand for as women: stories that capture our imaginations, stories that inspire, and stories that cultivate connections.

My story

My story echoes the stories of many Baby Boomer women who sought to shape an identity for themselves as working women. Feminists like Germaine Greer, Gloria Steinem and, my favourite, Marilyn French, author of the international bestseller *The Women's Room*, paved the way for me. The women's movement in Australia had begun the fight to embed laws of equal opportunity so I could participate in the workplace unencumbered by discrimination and sexual harassment. I commenced university with a strong sense that the world was open to me and that I could have it all — whatever that meant — certainly a life beyond domesticity or cleaning other peoples' houses and working in low-paid menial jobs, as my mother had. We were migrants and, for my mother, survival meant putting aside the hopes and dreams that she might have had as a beautiful and intelligent young girl growing up in pre-Holocaust Europe and accepting her new life in Australia with no English and no money. My father did not work. He had been the son of a wealthy European family and could never come to terms with his lost status post-Holocaust. My mother held the fort.

I arrived at university in the seventies not knowing what I wanted to do. I was good at maths and someone suggested I study economics. It was a way to understand the world. What could be measured could be managed. So I undertook an Honours degree in economics and econometrics — loved it, and followed it up with a Master's degree. I had pedigree qualifications and the world was my oyster.

After completing my degree at Monash University, I sent off a couple of job applications, confident that my strong degree would be highly sought after. Not so lucky. I must have chosen badly as I received responses unashamedly informing me that the organisation did not offer graduate positions to women. I should have kept the letters as archival evidence. Instead, I threw them out in disgust. I was learning about a world that discriminated on the basis of gender.

I applied for a job in the public service where, as a woman graduate and married woman, I could hope for a career path. It wasn't until 1966 that married women could work in the Commonwealth public service.[4] I worked in economic modelling and helped prepare the economic case for national wage cases.

I learnt very quickly that the world of organisations was complex, that the so-called rational world of economics operated in the context of a less rational world of people, power and industrial relations, where negotiating a good-enough settlement was not always the most efficient or economically viable. I began to understand what the philosopher David Hume meant when he wrote, 'Reason is the slave of passion.'

I also learnt that the 'Mad Men' era in which sexism and discrimination was overt and even celebrated extended beyond the '60s and well into the '70s and '80s. The era of sexual liberation had spilt over into the workplace, testing the limits of liberation and desire and blurring traditional codes of etiquette between the sexes. The boundary between sexual liberation and sexual harassment was increasingly confused. Behaviours that were kept underground or reserved for strictly men's circles surfaced as new norms. Offensive joking and put-downs, sexual innuendo and leering, were increasingly a part of the day-to-day life women (and some men) were contending with.

The *Sex Discrimination Act* was not introduced until in 1984. Prior to its introduction, there was little avenue for complaint. Sexual harassment was treated as 'trivial complaints about inharmonious working relationships, gripes about the personal proclivities of male workers that were unrelated to employers' responsibility, or whining about what was the inevitable sexual attractions that result from men and women working together'.[5]

Legislation may have curbed instances of overt sexism but it has not expunged discrimination or sexism from the workplace. Gender apartheid continues to persist with no good reason. Women are still trying to assert themselves as equal partners in the decision-making of this country and its organisations.

Sexism today is often more subtle, hidden and harder to identify. It can be shrouded in comedic levity, which makes it all the more difficult to deal with. Hence the furore when so-called benign, good-humoured advertising depicts women as stupid or as sexual objects or as both. However, not all sexism is hidden. The relentless humour directed at Australia's first female prime minister, Julia Gillard, has been neither hidden nor subtle. Political commentator Graham Morris's defence of his tweet that 'they ought to kick her to death' as just a quip, or broadcaster Alan Jones's response to his comment that Julia Gillard's father died of shame as 'black humour', is anything but humorous. The diet of verbal abuse meted out with impunity by male commentators and politicians — 'ditch the witch', 'deliberately barren', 'a menopausal monster', 'a lying cow' and 'political slut' — suggests a deep difficulty by some men with a woman at the helm. Gillard has not been the only victim of abuse directed at her because she is a woman. Today, one in five women experience sexual harassment, as do one in 20 men.

The 2012 *Australian Census for Women in Leadership*[6] indicates that the representation of women in Australian business leadership remains dismally low. That year, women represented only 3.8 percent of all the ASX 500 directors. Of the top 200 ASX companies, 65 still do not have women on their boards. The gender pay gap of 17 percent, costing $93 billion a year in lost productivity,[7] begins at graduate level, with female graduates earning almost 10 percent less than their male counterparts[8] and with the gap increasing the more senior a woman becomes. An educated woman can expect to earn 45 percent less than her male counterpart over her lifetime.

Sexism undermines women's confidence and resilience, as a recent University of Melbourne Centre for Ethical Leadership study reports.[9] Sadly, many women internalise cultures of hostility and lose confidence. In a climate that excludes women and judges them on a higher, harder and more shifting standard, women experience what has been coined *the imposter syndrome*: 'I'm sitting in this meeting room but I don't belong here.' If women are busy negotiating unsafe, hostile or over-scrutinising environments, it detracts from their capacity to engage as equals: to feel confident, to be productive and to flourish.

The motherhood juggle

I had married early, at 19, and my vision of a future was one that included children. My first child was born in 1983. By this stage I had left the government sector and joined private enterprise as a senior economist. After the birth of my daughter I was fortunate to negotiate part-time work with my employer. The right to request flexibility or reduced hours was not enshrined into law until 2009.[10] However, when I returned to work a few months later, I found myself asked to photocopy documents for my full-time male colleagues.

The idea that women are 'second earners' and marginal workers who work around their parenting responsibilities fed into a culture that saw a woman's status diminished once she was a mother. It helps explain why, over the last 30 years, women continue to receive lower pay, are concentrated in more insecure part-time work and their work is regarded as less important.[11] The legacy of this situation creates mental models that see part-time status as mitigating organisational seniority.

I decided it was time to move on and took up a half-time university post as a lecturer in economics and industrial relations. The bonus for me was that the university provided childcare facilities. The idea that my daughter was close by eased the difficulty of my separation from her.

By the time my son was born two years later, I was lecturing to a postgraduate group of students mainly from industry and government. Many were enrolled in a new program the university was offering, 'organisation behaviour', and were taking my subject as an elective. These were a group of challenging students with interesting perspectives that I was drawn to. I decided that I too would become a student of organisation behaviour.

If organisations are to nurture authentic female authority, there must also be zero tolerance for discrimination and harassment.

However, when I applied to enrol in the program, I was rejected on the grounds that I was a part-time employee at the university and the program at the business school was only open to full-time employees. Needless to say, there were more males than females in the program and the women did not have children. I mounted an internal discrimination case and won, and was able to enrol in the program in my status as a part-time employee.

The organisation behaviour program had an enormous impact on my understanding of organisational life, my career choices and the doctorate that I undertook years later. I had learnt early in my career, while working as an economist in the realpolitik of the Australian industrial relations system, that the world was only partly explainable by hard data, numbers and economic analyses. I now felt I had some added tools for making sense of phenomena that appeared at the outset to be inconsistent and irrational. I was now on a journey to appreciate paradoxes, deeper motivations and unconscious dynamics that were part of the reality of organisational life.

When my children were still very young, well before school age, I returned to full-time work and joined the private sector in strategic HR. I juggled work and family with the help of a string of nannies and wonderful girlfriends who picked up my children from preschool and school, fed them and loved them and still do. I am eternally grateful for their friendship and support.

The blokey world

I worked in steel, food, construction and the media industries. These were traditional male industries in a climate beset with industrial relations problems. It was a tough gig in the '80s and '90s, but I enjoyed the challenge and sought to make a difference to the cultures. They were hierarchical, inflexible, competitive and, in the main, adversarial, bifurcating management and workers, men and women, and Australians (anyone who was not in the most recent migrant group) and non-Australians. Cultures were also rampantly sexist, often under the guise of assistance. I recall a manager who pulled me aside to suggest that I abandon the pants suit, which was my daily office attire, for short skirts, which would 'show a bit more leg'. His demeanour was not lewd or sleazy. He considered himself a supporter of mine and his proffered advice, though misguided, was to assist me in navigating the workplace. Benign paternalism can be difficult to recognise, let alone deal with, but it has the same effect of making the target uncomfortable. I continued to wear pantsuits.

Relationships between women can also suffer in masculine cultures where women's sense of power is diminished and women's survival depends on serving male patrons and accommodating cultures rather than setting cultural agendas and challenging environments.[12] I was not immune from occasional dynamics that left me hurt and abandoned. But I was also rewarded with the strong bonds, support and counsel that women bring to their relationships. Susie Orbach and Luise Eichenbaum commented some 20 years ago that 'women's relationships produce a rainbow of powerful emotions'.[13] When harnessed and reflected upon, relationships provide the basis for our learning, for cementing our values and for redefining our role in the family and the workplace.

Something has to give

As long as everything at home went smoothly and nannies were in plentiful supply, then life was manageable. But when my son became ill I could no longer continue as I had. I left corporate life. It took months for him to fully recover and once again take part in full school activities.

I needed time out to reflect on what was possible for me as a mother and a professional. How was I going to lead my life for next few years? Organisations were generally inflexible for women who wanted to combine senior careers and part-time work. I did what many women do: I chose to set up my consulting business where I could work more flexibly. I realised, like many others, that 'having it all came at too much of a cost'. Even so, my children believe I worked too hard and wished I had been more like the mums who were actively involved in canteen duty, classroom activity and being there to pick their children up from school.

Today, flexibility options have improved dramatically. However, many women still drop out of careers during child-rearing years. Our culture continues to place responsibility for managing family squarely in the domain of women's work. When Julia Gillard, as prime minister, made the statement, 'I chose work over family', she was conveying a message to Australia that family and career at senior levels were mutually exclusive. Indeed, to be trusted to run the country or to run an organisation, a women needs be unencumbered by the demands of family.

Women who choose 'career' are less likely than their male counterparts to marry and have children. A 2001 survey reported that 49 percent of women defined as 'ultra-achieving career women' were childless (as opposed to 19 percent of men in the

same category) and 57 percent of 'high-achieving career women'
were unmarried (as opposed to 17 percent of males in the
same category).[14]

The economic imperative

The opportunity costs for business and society of an
underutilisation of female talent, as reported in a Goldman
Sachs study,[15] are immense. The study found that closing the gap
between male and female employment would boost Australia's
GDP by 11 percent.

By the 1990s, Australia was heading well towards becoming
an increasingly competitive, outward-looking, independent and
deregulated economy. The Karpin report[16] had highlighted the
lack of diversity in Australian business culture and the detrimental
effect this was having on relationships with trading partners.
Australia needed to embrace diversity more effectively. Yet cultural
practices and economic structures continually reinforce the
subjugation of women in society.

By the late 1990s, the Australian economy was experiencing an
unprecedented period of prosperity and growth, and the shortage
of skilled labour was being identified as a key factor restraining
growth: the 'war on talent' was truly on. Gender diversity had been
a moral concern and an academic concern, but it was now gaining
traction as an economic concern. Organisations were not able to
attract and retain talent in sufficient numbers to meet the demands
of a thriving economy. Women were beginning to be recognised as
a valuable but underutilised resource that needed to be tapped. But
capturing female talent was proving difficult.

By this time I was working for an eclectic client base in the
area of leadership and governance, areas in which women's

representation was lamentably low despite laudable attempts by a number of corporates to increase the representation of women at senior ranks. Conversations with business leaders led to my being commissioned by a number of organisations from the corporate, government and tertiary sectors to undertake a major research project[17] to better understand barriers to attracting and retaining female talent by exploring the experiences of men and women in organisations, particularly as it related to progressing into leadership positions.

Leadership — a masculine enterprise

What did I find? My overarching conclusion was that leadership was a masculine enterprise. The structure of work had progressed little since the 1950s, leadership roles demanded 24/7 availability, and the look and feel of leadership was masculine — as in 'think leader, think male'. Women and power form an uneasy alliance. Five years later, in 2011, I continued the line of inquiry and partnered in a research project with the Committee for Economic Development of Australia (CEDA). The findings of our consequent report, 'Women in Leadership: Looking below the Surface',[18] indicate that despite commitment and targets, and indeed significant progress made in organisations, dynamics both conscious and unconscious continue to perpetuate situations that reinforce the status quo that sees women underrepresented in leadership and their contributions undervalued.

While the rhetoric of business may have shifted from 'women are the problem and women need to change' to 'organisations are the problem and organisations need to change', the lingering message continues to suggest that women are lacking what it takes to get to the top. Women continue to be bombarded with well-meaning suggestions that if only they changed their behaviour, their problems would be resolved. Women should be more assertive and they should negotiate harder. Women have also been advised that they should use fewer words in their communication if they want to be heard, based on a now-debunked myth that men use fewer words. Research shows that women's attempts to speak up and to negotiate harder are unlikely to produce the desired outcomes.[19] The same behaviours that raise a man's status make a woman less popular. When women display ambition, they risk the backlash of being seen as aggressive and masculine. Yet if they are collaborative and communal they are viewed as weak — the classic double bind.

Organisations operate in two parallel universes: the idealised, articulated part that understands the business case and promotes gender equality; and a more primitive, hidden and unconscious part that sits beyond conscious awareness and sees patriarchy reinforced and women's status undermined. Both men and women are stuck in a holding pattern of male dominance and collectively collude in a belief system that systemically discriminates against women and diminishes female authority.

David Thodey, Managing Director of Telstra and a member of Elizabeth Broderick's Champions for Change group[20] that has engaged senior male business leaders to elevate the status of women in leadership,' was quoted as saying:

> 'Gender bias is about culture and an environment of inclusion ... I feel frustrated as a leader and dissatisfied with the progress we have made ... I know it's a leadership issue and I know we don't have the answers.'[21]

Thodey's acknowledgment of not knowing, of not having the

answers, of not being in control, is perhaps a good starting point for discovery, for challenging the status quo in an effort to shift paradigms. A paradigm shift is needed in order to see sustainable change in the status of women in our society. As long as the alignment between women and authority, and between men and family responsibility, remains fragile, women will continue to be marginalised in the workplace.

The way forward

To move forward we need to shift deeply ingrained cultures in which there is an uneasy alliance between women and power. We need to challenge stereotypical thinking about what it means to be a leader. We need to shift cultures that reinforce unpalatable cultural stereotypes that impede a true partnership between men and women in the workplace and in the family. This requires a concerted effort from leadership at the highest levels — corporates, media, government and sport — to rethink what progress really means and to build inclusive visions for the future of our organisations and societies. Leaders have a far-reaching influence footprint and must use their voices to not only address inequity in their own organisations but also advocate for gender equality in the public domain. They must act now. No leader can be a silent bystander.

For patriarchy to be expunged, however, women must also take up active leadership. As women, we need to be mindful of our own collusion in systems that marginalise us. Simone de Beauvoir wrote:

'Representation of the world, like the world itself, is the work of men. They describe it from their own point of view, which they confuse with absolute truth.' [22]

According to a recent Catalyst study, women seek acceptance by 'developing a style with which male managers are comfortable'. Indeed, women collude 'by protecting men from their femininity, complicatedness and distraction'.[23]

As women, we need to transcend the male perspective by seeing ourselves with fresh eyes:

> 'Only when a woman's vision is cleared of cultural and self-imposed limitations that emanate from that culture will she have access to the missing half of the human puzzle — her beliefs, her values, her goals, her style, her way of doing things.'[24]

As women, we need to find our voices to convey our way of doing things. We need to tell our stories and share our journeys. We need to advocate for one another. We need to inspire each other to aspire to great things. We need to celebrate our achievements, not as the exceptions reserved for 'extraordinary women', but as norms accessible to women for the great and mostly silent contributions women make to create a better world.

Dr Kerry Baxter

Against the Odds

Dr Kerry Baxter has completed a research PhD on women's career development in corporate organisations in the financial services industry. Her dissertation, 'Leading Ladies: The Power of Passion', found that, contrary to popular belief, women do want to lead. They believe they can lead and they do lead; however, their journey to the top is fundamentally different from the traditional corporate career model.

Kerry has over 30 years of professional experience as a senior executive in the corporate world, and is currently working as a management consultant and executive coach, encouraging organisations to have conversations and implement strategies that enable companies to thrive and employees to flourish.

Background to the research

Women in executive positions are still a novelty in many Australian corporate organisations. There are, however, a small number of women who, against the odds, do take up the challenge to lead and hold executive positions in corporate organisations.

The purpose of my research was to contribute to emergent and ongoing thought about the nature of women's career development in today's corporate organisations. When we take into account the benefits of gender diversity for organisations and society as a whole, it is paramount that we understand why women are still underrepresented in executive positions with corporate organisations.

What tantalised my curiosity, however, was: What can be learned from those women who do hold executive positions? I sought to explore this question by developing a rich picture of the career development journey of 12 women who held executive positions within the Australian financial services industry. Secondly, what, if anything, can organisations do to support the emergence of a corporate environment that will attract and retain professional women so as to optimise the contribution of talented women in executive leadership? I argue that, despite the significant gains made by women in the workforce over the last few decades, very little has changed for women in executive leadership. While many studies are concerned with the barriers to women's professional advancement, this study was primarily concerned with exploring what is possible for professional women.

The study

As Heraclitus, the Greek philosopher, remarked: 'You cannot step twice into the same river, for fresh waters are ever flowing in upon you.'[1] We cannot keep looking at the same phenomenon through the same lens and expect to see something different. Organisations as social contexts are never the same; they are in a continual state of flux. Therefore, I sought to transcend our current understanding of women and work in an empirical study informed by complexity. Complexity[2] provides the overarching logic, methodological approach, technique and primary metaphors through which the findings are articulated and elaborated. Building on the valuable work of those who have researched this subject before, and focusing on the organisation and the factors that shape women's career development, I determined that institutional changes aimed at improving women's representation in executive positions have not led to significant change and suggest that complexity provides a new understanding that goes beyond the prevailing views of stereotypical and cultural barriers obstructing women's career advancement.

From conversations with 12 women in executive positions about their everyday experience in corporate organisations, I wanted to understand what could be learned from those women who do hold executive positions. More specifically, I wanted to understand:

- What are the organisational factors and experiences that shape these women's corporate careers?

- Why are so few women being designated executive leadership positions?

- Are women's organisational careers being constrained by unconscious prejudices around capabilities and social expectations?

- What are these women's success factors?

I discovered these women were all driven by the same four factors as they self-organised their corporate careers. Firstly, initial conditions influenced and shaped how these women constructed and thought about their career. Secondly, their career stories were strongly entwined with contexts such as society, family and the personal domain. Thirdly, the findings indicate that as these women shift seamlessly from one role to another they constructed temporary identities ('professional', 'mother', 'wife') as they followed their life cycle passions. Fourthly, the career journeys of the women were shown to be nonlinear and characterised as unpredictable and almost serendipitous as they changed course to make what I have termed 'passion leaps' at various times in their career. These leaps required risk-taking and foresight and an unbridled enthusiasm for an uncertain future and a not-so-certain landing. What emerged were women who were passionate about their positions and comfortable with leadership and taking executive positions; they just did it differently to men. Therefore, while the corporate environment must change in its behaviours, values and practices to fully support women's difference, this is not the whole story. The decision to lead is strongly influenced by the women themselves and the way they thought about their ability and the possibilities they envisioned for themselves.

My focus was on identifying what works and what could work, rather than what does not work. So, rather than look at why there are so few women in executive positions, I uncovered possibilities for new ways of thinking about women's careers.

Findings that lead to new beginnings

What motivated these women to take up executive positions? The study found that these women's individual career actions skipped around almost serendipitously and appeared unpredictable; they were driven by four interrelated and co-dependent attractors of meaning that influenced their behaviour and propelled them forward:

1. *Passion:* achievement, doing what they loved, learning and passion leaps.

2. *Identity:* confidence, courageous, values and differentiated optimistic attitude.

3. *Freedom:* counter-suggestive, opportunistic, managed risks and self-directed.

4. *Connection:* family, networks, relationship mutuality and support.

Let's look at these four attractors some more.

1. Passion

Passion is about doing what they loved with energy and optimism. They expressed a strong desire to achieve and that desire was fuelled by a passion that supported the expression of their personal values and varying expectations of career success. Passion motivated them to do what they loved to do. Moving forward often required them to make what I have termed 'passion leaps': leaps made out of a genuine passion to do something, based on strong intuition. These women backed themselves — they saw no impediment to success and going backwards was not an option. This mindset enabled them to make apparent random career leaps like a spider's web that crisscrossed in and around their own contexts: families, industries, corporations, different businesses and roles.

This passion created in them a vision that often compelled them into a dynamic and unpredictable future. These actions suggest that they were not slaves to the idea that the corporate environment was the only place to have a career. While they noted that the corporate world was alluring and often hard to leave for a number of reasons, when changes occurred within the environment that were not coherent with their identity, these things were not enough to keep them. They were happy to adapt and make small changes to fit into the organisation, but when the environment no longer held any meaning for them or it became inconsistent with their values, they moved to another position or environment — this was a 'passion leap'. Risk-taking was a common theme among the women, almost as if they thrived on the non-established order or unpredictability of the next move.

Making these 'passion leaps' generally meant a different and dynamic route to the top. For these women, there were no corporate ladders to be climbed. Taking their own path enabled them to bypass much of the traffic jam on the metaphorical ladder and avoid the resistance that many women report coming up against in the middle of the corporate career ladder. In fact, nine of the women reflected that, on more than one occasion, they did not expect to see a glass ceiling — and they did not. With no expectation of a glass ceiling, they adapted to whatever came along. Any resistance that was encountered was managed like any other problem: it would either be mutually resolved or they would adapt accordingly. The key here is that they were confident in their ability to choose other options.

2. Identity

All the women in my research had a strong self-image and belief in their ability. They understood the need to remain true to this self-image and identity while continually self-organising across changing circumstances and contexts over time. This self-image was the basis upon which they made informed choices and decisions in relation to their careers and within their social, organisational and family contexts. The role as an executive position within a corporate organisation contributed to these women's sense of autonomy and personal and professional identity.

These women were different to other leaders. Optimistic, courageous and values-driven, they differentiated themselves as leaders who, with a strong self-belief, used their voice and used it confidently, challenging ideas or decisions to find mutually suitable solutions. When their identity was perceived to be under threat, they took action — which sometimes involved leaving the corporate arena.

Generally, these participants were clear about their values and life priorities. They demonstrated personal responsibility for managing their own careers; they prioritised their time so they could fulfil their differing life cycle commitments in a way that was aligned with their values and committed priorities. Their capacity to manage their identity and their corporate careers was sustained when they could maintain their passionate participation in doing what they loved to do at work and by being part of an environment that was conducive to maintaining good relationships.

Actively managing their own career identities was strongly influenced by their counter-suggestive nature, in that they wanted to ensure that any societal and cultural views of women's roles and the taking of executive positions were not forced upon them. It could be said that the women in this study were able to create their own corporate executive identity because of their access to resources. Having their basic human needs met, they were able to access the additional resources that their socioeconomic status provided: freedom of choice, access to education, networks and relational support. All of these encouraged their growth and identification as professional women who could follow their passion: a passion that led them to executive leadership.

3. *Freedom*

Being motivated by a passion for doing what you love, having dreams and aspirations, means nothing if you do not have the freedom to pursue them. Freedom is generally understood as the power or right to act, speak or think as one wants without hindrance or restraint. As Gandhi said, 'Freedom has to be taken,' and these women took their freedom. They created their own freedom through their thoughts and actions. They thought differently, often courageously challenging the status quo. They were opportunistic, managed risks and were highly self-directed. From a career perspective they expressed their desire for freedom in the way they approached their work and in the decisions they made, where they worked and, most importantly for these women, with whom they worked. The degree of freedom they sought meant their long-term career plans were unpredictable, unconventional and full of variety, which did pose a number of constraints and challenges such as the lack of financial security and the need to quickly rebuild their credibility in a new environment while building new alliances and a supportive network of relationships. These constraints and challenges required resilience and creativity, which came rather naturally to them because of their counter-suggestive nature, as discussed above. They often expressed a love for solving problems and excitement about achieving a challenge that someone suggested that they could not do. They were energised by constraints and enabled by their passion for learning. Learning enabled them to change and adapt their behaviour according to the changing circumstances.

The women mostly orchestrated their own career opportunities. They sought the freedom and the power to make their own decisions, and were self-directed and curious as they followed their own compass, which appeared to serendipitously lead them to an executive leadership position. What I think is interesting and different about these women was how comfortable they were in making their choices around the opportunities they created. Their life cycle priorities and values had a strong influence on their career priorities and the career positions they took within and outside the organisations they worked for. Regardless of context, their counter-suggestive nature often found them rubbing up against something or someone who said they could not or should not do something differently. This did not deter them; rather, the challenge and the friction actually spurred them on to prove they could do it, while proving the alternative suggestion less effective, and the friction created an opportunity for something new and unpredictable to emerge. They appeared to thrive on the competitive nature of the challenge.

The issue of women taking time out of the corporate workplace to have a child is often seen as a lack of commitment to a corporate career, the implications being that it made it exceedingly difficult to re-join. This was not the case for these women. They chose to leave the corporate environment for a myriad of reasons, yet they were still clearly committed to their workplace leadership and exercising their power constructively when they were in those positions. Going against the trend found in other research,[3] I found no significant detrimental issues were highlighted as a result of them leaping in and out of their corporate positions. Perhaps this occurred because they were comfortable exercising the power to move in and out of the corporate environment, or perhaps because of their optimistic attitude they did not expect to be faced with any issues and therefore did not see any. Being comfortable about their actions did not imply that they did not face challenges or problems in the workplace. They did. Well-educated and having the capacity and willingness to solve problems, they did solve them and they then supported the decisions that emerged.

4. Connection

The women in this study were connected: they contributed and belonged to families, networks and organisations. Being connected does not arise from nowhere. Each of the women talked about the influence of their historical and present relationships and the nature and quality of those relationships. Within a family context, 12 of the participants had a family, 11 had children, and nine of the participants described the support, encouragement and a mutually empowering relationship with their partners as an integral part of their ability to follow their passion and take a corporate executive position.

Their careers, while often appearing to progress through chance, coincidence or serendipity, were always a result of the connections they made. They regularly referred to tapping into their internal resources (self-direction and determination) to get things done or their external connections (such as the networks that they created from many different origins) that validated, supported and encouraged them. Moreover, they repeatedly discussed how growth-fostering work relationships were central to their career actions.

Women's networks were actively fostered by several of the women because they found these to be engaging, hopeful, rewarding and mutually beneficial. One woman used the phrase 'women whispers' to express what women do well but many do not do enough of. 'Women whisperers' are like-minded women who build collaborative networks of relationships across all contexts that support, encourage, share knowledge and have fun with one another. Growth and learning relationships were identified as important to these women's career choices, so it is not surprising that these participants chose to network.

Additionally, their corporate connections and relationships were dynamic; they were formed, broken and reformed over time, within a web of social and cultural contexts. Their career journeys were filled with disconnection as they moved away from corporate life to pursue other life goals or move toward different connections and career experiences. They disconnected and reconnected to relationships and networks, as they needed. They did not suffer from the wanting of career opportunity; they had the personal drive, freedom, socioeconomic status and relational support to enable them to create their own career opportunities. For these women, connection was a key self-organising factor in their career creation. The strong desire for connection revolved around an intention to interact and build networks in an environment that supported mutuality in relationships (specifically, with their immediate manager). Relationships really mattered to these women; they affected the potentiality of their actions: where they worked, when they worked, whom they worked with and how they worked. If their local relationships were good, they would stay in the organisations, often regardless of any gendered or unhealthy corporate cultures. If bad, they left. I suggest that, rather than a commitment to a particular organisation, they were committed to the relationships around them.

The concept of possibility

Viewing the world and experience as complex enables a different paradigm around what is possible. This way of viewing the world allows greater richness of experience and freedom for conceiving of 'other' future possibilities.[4]

Complex systems do not 'know in advance' where they are going; rather, they seem to be pushed or pulled around in accordance with certain rules. The women in this study reflected on how they did not set out with a specific goal to take an executive position within a corporate organisation; they did, however, have an intention to actively seek out opportunities to do what they loved to do. For these women, leadership was emergent. Taking an executive position in a corporate organisation was contextual and negotiated around life-cycle choices; it was self-directed and opportunistic.

It is very important at this point to reiterate that it was the women themselves who defined their leadership position as 'success'. Often this success was described by the participants as coincidental, accidental or serendipitous. However, there is more than coincidence and serendipity here; there is the ability to nudge or influence their own success. They made a choice to adapt and succeed in the corporate environment, and the underlying rules that guided their actions supported their success. Context- and time-dependent, their success did not always emerge in the corporate organisation; there were times when their life-cycle passions or priorities led them to make 'passion leaps' that took them out of the corporate organisation and into other environments.

What can we learn from these women? Here are 15 simple recurrent rules (behaviours) of interaction that governed their success behaviour and how they got things done:

1. They made 'passion leaps' to follow their passion and do what they loved to do.

2. Relationships really mattered.

3. They chose success and achieved results.

4. They orchestrated their own career opportunities.

5. Their careers were relational and context-dependent.

6. They managed and took risks.

7. They were in action — had a 'can-do attitude'.

8. They were connected — they were supported.

9. Learning was reflexive and continual.

10. They networked: they were 'women whisperers'.

11. The way they perceived the world influenced the results they got.

12. Their leadership careers were emergent, self-organised and dynamic — serendipitous.

13. They had strong self-belief.

14. An optimistic attitude.

15. They adapted to the paradoxical aspects of a corporate environment.

These women's engagement in the corporate organisations was internally motivated. In other words, their success had a lot to do with their focused attitude and personal effort to give their best and to thrive in the environment they chose to work in. Despite having the intention of success as well as confident and competent delivery of action, there was no guarantee of success. These women kept looking for success; they looked for positive matches and ways to fit in. They survived by continually filtering for positive outcomes. Unpredictable events occurred, issues emerged, and they managed them; their reflective ability to seek alternative forms of action when previous actions failed was enhanced by a mindset of continual learning.

They were continually challenged to adjust to new contexts and new roles, yet these women survived. Taking and applying this knowledge will not automatically guarantee success in a different time and in a different context. Leaders emerge in a wide variety of circumstances and reflect a broad range of talent and personalities. There is no one pattern of behaviour or personality type most suitable for the leadership role.[5] We can influence in the right direction, but we have to walk the path ourselves. However, understanding and being aware of the self-organisational dynamics of these women's corporate careers does provide valuable insight on how to remove the obstacles for organisations and women seeking an executive position with a corporate organisation.

It is possible that the above list of 15 success factors could equally apply to men pursuing career success. However, in keeping with the research conventions characterising rigorous and trustworthy research, it is inappropriate for me to make such claims here.

Summary and conclusions

'We are what we think having become what we thought.'
— *Pavithra*

Contrary to conventional wisdom, this research identified that the women who participated in this study do want to lead, and they were very comfortable with power and holding an executive position within a corporate organisation. What makes these women's stories interesting is their motivation for taking executive positions within the corporate space and their ability to handle the paradoxical nature of organisational life. The majority of participants were not motivated by position or the status attributed to an executive position. Nine of the women reported that it was more important for them to make a difference by developing and growing people and a successful business. By being part of the corporate system and taking an executive position, they were able to do this. However, they were not slaves to the idea that the corporate organisation was the only place for them to achieve. These women were just as comfortable taking leading roles outside the corporate organisation.

This research shows that, generally, women's careers develop in fundamentally different ways from the traditional model of career development, which creates a climate of competition for the next position through a time-served, status-driven hierarchy.

These women's career journeys could not be delegated to someone else to manage. Their leadership was self-organised, dynamic and emergent, in a forward-moving process; it was full of connections and relationships. My findings suggest that women do want to lead and have a corporate career; they just need and want to do it differently. These women demonstrated that they are leading in a more collaborative and inclusive way that establishes communicative connectedness to achieve business success.

Describing themselves as successful on their own terms, these women lived passionately and powerfully and, like many other Western women, they live and work in a dynamic society that is full of societal expectation and contradictory behaviours towards women holding executive positions. My research found, as others[6] also have, that the lack of women at the top of corporate organisations has little to do with their lack of ability or interest in holding executive leadership positions in corporate organisations. Nor does it have to do with their choices to leap out of the corporate organisation for other life priorities, such as parenting. I propose that it has more to do with the way work is organised, the relationships that are formed, together with the subtle, but deeply held, gender assumptions that continue to shape models of the corporate career, leadership and leaders.

The women who participated in this research were ordinary women: women doing what they loved and doing it successfully. They faced the everyday challenges of society, organisations, family and the personal domain with a strong belief in their own capacity to influence and achieve the important aspects of their life. They worked in corporate organisations that were systemically dysfunctional and experienced work cultures that were not terribly inclusive or supportive of gender diversity. However, they chose success and, with that intention, created a life full of opportunities and possibilities that supported their taking of executive positions. They wanted to lead, they believed they could lead, and they did lead, passionately and differently from many other men and women. I am grateful and thankful for their contribution, because they provide glowing examples of what is possible for professional women.

It is my hope that this new understanding will support the emergence of a different career model and ways of defining corporate career success and working in the corporate organisation. This difference may well support the inclusion of women and the valuing of what women have to offer: their ways of working and doing things so that they are engaged and retained in corporate organisations, thus enabling them to be involved in the decision-making of those organisations.

10 Inspirational Stories
of Career Success

Katie Lahey

Grab that Opportunity

 From humble beginnings as a shoe-shop assistant, Yorkshire-born Katie came to Australia, aged 21, on a three-year working holiday and rose to become one of the most senior women in Australian business circles. Prior to joining Korn/Ferry, of which she is now Managing Director, Katie was the Chief Executive of the Business Council of Australia (BCA), an association of the chief executive officers of Australia's 100 largest companies. Before joining the BCA in 2001, she held CEO roles in the State Chamber of Commerce (New South Wales), Sydney City Council and the Victorian Tourism Commission from 1989 to 1992. In 2003, Katie was awarded a Centenary Medal for her contribution to Australian society in the area of business leadership.

Major Turning Points

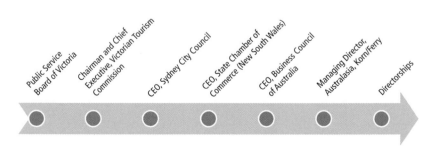

Public Service Board of Victoria

Chairman and Chief Executive, Victorian Tourism Commission

CEO, Sydney City Council

CEO, State Chamber of Commerce (New South Wales)

CEO, Business Council of Australia

Managing Director, Australasia, Korn/Ferry

Directorships

Katie combines a deft touch and wicked sense of humour with a commanding intellect and shrewd knowledge of how businesses and organisations work at the most senior levels. When you talk with Katie you are immediately set at ease with her gracious and inviting conversational style. She makes the journey to the top of one of the premier executive search firms and as director on some of Australia's leading boards sound deceptively effortless.

'Work hard, don't let anything stand in your way'

Katie hails from Yorkshire and reflects on some early character-forming experiences in her upbringing with fondness and deep appreciation. She draws her strong practical streak from her mother, whose motto was, 'Work hard, don't let anything stand in your way, Katie.' She herself was an incredibly hard worker who combined a job with bringing up four children under eight while Katie's father was posted overseas with the navy. Katie recounted a time when her father was in the Gulf somewhere and a message came through that he'd been posted to the north of Scotland; her mother moved the family up to Scotland on her own to join him. She was a bright, intelligent woman, although not tertiary-educated, and was very supportive of her children gaining an education. With no extended family and their father at sea, the children weren't allowed to have days off sick from school. Katie can recall many a time being sent home from school and thinking, 'Mmm, my mother's not there. I'd better put myself to bed.'

Katie also credits her mother with a positive philosophy on life and with learning the benefits of rewarding herself. Her mother would pose the question, 'Katie, if you can't afford it, who can?' and gave her a marvellous appreciation of the importance in a woman's life of being able to treat oneself. As a director of David

Jones, Katie follows this philosophy today to understand what female consumers are looking for and the benefits of retail therapy. Although she recently stepped down from the David Jones board, Katie remains a totally committed shopaholic.

Her relationship with her mother was pivotal in her understanding of herself and her potential in life, yet ironically the decision to leave her mother and her homeland presented the first turning point in Katie's career. Her first husband, an electrical engineer, couldn't get work in the UK, so they decided to emigrate and Katie arrived in Australia on a three-year working holiday.

'That job's mine': being an opportunist and trusting instinct

'If there's a wonderful opportunity and it's going past my door, I'm going to grab it.'

Katie's first job in Australia was as an accounts clerk. When it was clear that Australia was going to be her long-term home, she completed a Bachelor of Arts (Honours) at the University of Melbourne, joining the Victorian Public Service as a graduate trainee. Katie described her advancement through the public service and into leadership roles as a result of following her instinct when opportunities present. Breadth has been a driver for her: she has pursued roles in all three tiers of government as well as in not-for-profit and profit-making companies, in large and small organisations, and in Victoria and New South Wales. Katie explains that she recognised many of these as great opportunities to be taken with both hands and describes herself as 'absolutely the opportunistic person'. Each of her five CEO roles has been completely different but she is a big believer in the generalist, rather than the technical specialist, career. For her, a job needs human contact, and she likes the juggling and the opportunity to be working on half a dozen things at the same time with a team.

Before she accepted the role at Korn/Ferry, many people expected her to take board positions — something she had been doing with many organisations for 20 years. But, in the end, she relishes getting her hands dirty and being out and about with something she is held accountable for. If you're the CEO, there is no doubt about where the accountability lies.

Higher education was another defining moment of opportunity for Katie, who was offered the chance to study for an MBA while working with the Victorian Government. She was a public servant 'who had never even read *The Financial Review*' and ended up at the top of her class. Ever the opportunist, Katie describes this period as completely mind-opening. She studied with classmates from the alien private sector just as the stock market was crashing around them, and watched with fascination as the class gripped their seats. Despite revelling in the opportunity, this was not an easy time for her, as she had to step up to the role of Acting CEO when her boss was forced to take extended sick leave.

Katie is also a firm believer in trusting her gut instinct. After nine years as Chief Executive Officer of the Business Council of Australia (BCA), just as she was thinking it might be time to move on, she was approached by Korn/Ferry to be its CEO. The firm assured her there would need to be an extended due diligence process on both sides. At nine o'clock the next day, Katie rang to say, 'That job's mine,' and she laughed about how her instinct overtook the due diligence she should have been adhering to. But, she told herself, it was a people job; it would draw on her extended networks built through the BCA, and she knew something of the processes, procedures and protocols of executive search from her human resources background and own personal experience on the other side of the fence. Interestingly, when the news broke, many people commented on what good sense the move made. Currently, she is finding her new role a complex one as she leads a large partnership with many and varied perspectives involved in the decision-making, but she considers this a challenge to relish.

Keep moving forward

Katie's career has been unmarked by spectacular falls from grace or being out in the cold. Unfailingly optimistic as she is, Katie had to be pressed to share a view on the tougher times. However, there was a period of great disappointment earlier in her career. As Deputy of the Department of Property and Service, she applied for the Head of Department position when it became vacant and was very disappointed to lose the role to a male appointee. At 39, this was the first time Katie had ever put her hand up for something unsuccessfully. She was devastated and 'behaved like a dog with a sore head for three months'. The wise counsel of a friend pulled her out of her obsession with this loss and persuaded her to focus on looking for her next role. This turned out to be as head of the Victorian Tourism Commission, a job she thought was 10 times better. If she had allowed herself to continue to be eaten up by the loss of the other role, this one could easily have passed her by. The lesson Katie took from this experience and now shares with others is: if you do get knocked back, don't let the bitterness show, as it reverberates on to others and, significantly, can stop you from focusing on where to head next.

Can't do it on your own

Katie honours her public sector bosses of 30 years ago who were not afraid to employ, support and encourage women in their careers many years before it was considered natural or appropriate to do so. She speaks of Bill Russell, who made her his Deputy in the Department of Property and Services. He was open to new ideas and really encouraged her to put herself forward. Other important figures along the way include Elizabeth Proust, with whom she worked at the Public Service Board, and, at the Business Council, people she describes as some of the best chairmen in Australia: John Schubert, Hugh Morgan, Michael Chaney, Graham Bradley and Greg Gailey.

She also is convinced that a happy home life is really important and that both parties in a relationship should be willing and able to be flexible in order for each other's careers to flourish, although she talks ruefully of the logistical challenges of managing domestic affairs. Recognising that the nirvana of work–life balance is elusive at the top levels, Katie emphasises the value of having someone at home with whom you can be completely frank and honest. Her husband, Rob, holds the leadership human resources role at the Bank of Tokyo, and she admits that it is tough at times to manage the demands of two high-level corporate careers. She attributes their success in making it work to their shared ability to be flexible; when she took the CEO role at Sydney City Council, he found himself as the trailing spouse and Katie remarked that at no point did he take umbrage at this. However, when it came to the Business Council of Australia role, Rob wanted to stay put in Sydney, despite being a Melburnian, as he was enjoying his job. It was Katie's turn to be flexible and she commuted from Sydney.

How do you be a woman in a man's world?

'Who wouldn't rather spend a night in than going out and doing another networking cocktail party? But you don't get to the top by being a recluse.'

Katie believes that an underlying discrimination still exists, reflected by the fact that women are still in the minority in more senior roles in companies and on boards, and she believes that women still find it harder to reach success than men. However, Katie does acknowledge that she has never thought that she didn't get a job because she was a woman.

In each of her CEO roles, she has been the first woman CEO, all of them in male-dominated environments. Often, she recounted, the novelty value of having a woman in those roles made it a bit easier. The men had no experience of women at that level, so in many ways it was a help rather than a hindrance because she could set the ground rules and do things her way with no comparisons for others to make.

Absolutely fundamental to success, she believes, is the practice of networking and pushing yourself to do it. She recalls that her first discussion about her seat on the David Jones board was by chance when she was sitting next to somebody influential over a dinner. She encourages women who are considering board memberships to embrace networking deliberately as a project, arguing that, if they take on projects in their everyday job, then networking should be one of them. Her advice to any woman who thinks she is too busy is that it probably only takes two lunches and one evening out a month. Very few people, she points out, get to the top by being a recluse.

'What I know now': lessons for her younger self

'Other people don't need to beat us up because we spend so much energy doing that ourselves.'

As Katie reflects on the progress of her career she shares a personal motto to never look backward. While there are lessons to be learnt from the past, her counsel to women is that you can spend a lot of time dwelling on things that might have been, could have been, could have been done better, could have been said ... but in the end this wastes a lot of time. Women, she believes, spend a lot of time beating themselves up unnecessarily. Better to make mistakes, accept them, and move on; dwelling can only sap your confidence.

Katie believes that staying true to your own values is critical and, importantly, that your company's values and your own need to be in sync. She has watched people in leadership roles where this is not the case and she can spot the internal stress that follows. Taking the business to the next level is important for Katie, but only if this progress is managed in a way that she characterises as dignified. 'Crash or crash through' is an approach she is uncomfortable with and considers unsophisticated, preferring a change that takes a little longer but leaves people's dignity intact.

Having fun matters, too, and a sense of humour helps. Katie acknowledges that she has a really good sense of humour. However, she sometimes has to watch herself, as what she might consider a joke or an off-the-cuff remark can inadvertently filter through the organisation and, before she realises it, become law.

Katie admits her frustration with communicating a vision without coming over like a motivational guru — something she has worked hard on for much of her career. In this regard, she considers that her Yorkshire roots might be less than helpful; the natives of Yorkshire are not renowned for their expressive natures or excitability, and Katie admits that she would have loved a bit more American showmanship with an ability to put herself centrestage.

What's next

'I do feel proud when I see young women where my path and theirs have crossed somewhere, and I hope I've given them a leg up and made a contribution to their success and their careers.'

Katie contemplates a path as a full-time company director as her next and final career move, but for her that would entail relinquishing her CEO role. She is very clear on the different roles of director and CEO, and ruefully acknowledges the temptation that arises in board discussions when she thinks, 'Ooh, I'd love to do that project. But I know I mustn't.' Refusing to get confused is, she believes, the hallmark of a good director.

Another source of joy will be continuing to mentor the next generation. Katie talks with fondness about seeing people she has coached and encouraged through the years, following in her footsteps. For Katie, there can be no greater pleasure than thinking that these women will someday be in her chair.

Ann Sherry, AO

Career Hopscotch

In 2001, Ann Sherry was awarded a Centenary Medal by the Australian Government for her work in providing banking services to disadvantaged communities.

In 2004, Ann was appointed an Officer of the Order of Australia (AO) for her contribution to the Australian community through the promotion of corporate management policies and practices that embrace gender equity, social justice, and work and family partnerships.

In 2009, Ann was nominated as one of the Top 15 Women in Business worldwide by the businesswomen's magazine *Pink*.

Major Turning Points

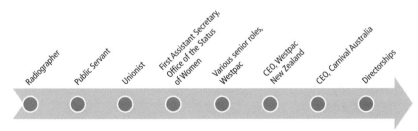

Radiographer — Public Servant — Unionist — First Assistant Secretary, Office of the Status of Women — Various senior roles, Westpac — CEO, Westpac New Zealand — CEO, Carnival Australia — Directorships

Ann Sherry's wide smile and genuine friendliness is a charming counterpart to her professional, no-nonsense aproach. Her ability to put people at ease makes business and personal discussions comfortable.

Anchors aweigh

As First Assistant Secretary of the Office of the Status of Women (OSW) from 1993 to 1994, Ann provided advice to then prime minister Paul Keating before taking the rather unique opportunity to make a successful transition out of the public sector into the corporate world. By the year 2000, she had been made Chief Executive Officer of the Bank of Melbourne (a division of Westpac) and within two years was CEO of Westpac New Zealand. She remained in this role for another five years, spending 13 years in all with Westpac. In 2007, she happened by chance to bump into a colleague in the rarefied world of female CEOs, Katie Lahey, who is also featured in this book. Their meeting set off a series of discussions and Ann was invited to be the CEO of Carnival Australia, the ailing but nevertheless strong backbone of Australia's cruise ship industry.

As with Westpac, Ann was the first woman to be appointed CEO of Carnival Australia despite being unfamiliar with the industry and not even living in the country. These sorts of dramatic career changes were not unusual for Ann, whose career began as a radiographer before she moved to the public service. She also had a stint as a trade unionist, then went back to government, banking and, now, tourism — 'bizarre moves', as Ann describes them.

While happenstance may have surrounded many of these career moves, there are two constant elements that keep coming up: her ability to embrace change and her passion to fight for what she believes in.

At Carnival Australia, Ann and her team defied the current global downturn and the flagging tourism industry, moving the business in the opposite direction to become the fastest-growing sector within tourism in Australia. The number of Australians travelling on Carnival cruise liners[1] increased from 80,000 in 2001 to 700,000 in 2011, with the target being one million by 2020 — a goal that is now easily within reach. Ann remembers that people thought she was 'completely bonkers' when she set these targets in 2007, but she believes that the point of setting huge targets was to get people to think differently and proactively about what was an otherwise stagnating business. The figures show she was right; however, her efforts were not all smooth sailing, if you will pardon the pun.

A shot across the bows

'I almost found my new self facing my old self.'

Who would have thought, least of all Ann, that she would end up disputing the very legislation she had been instrumental in initiating while with the OSW in 1994: the Commonwealth *Age Discrimination Act*? This Act, which was finally introduced 10 years later in 2004, made it unlawful in certain circumstances to discriminate against people on the basis of their age and protected people against age discrimination in many walks of life. It heralded a new era in the recognition of age discrimination in Australia.

When Ann began work with Carnival Australia, she made the decision to discontinue the specific 'schoolies cruises' offered over the summer months and any marketing aimed at school leavers. The company had been struggling with the increase in alcohol-related incidents during the traditional schoolies period, when high school graduates celebrate the end of high school, often to excess. However, these measures did not have much effect in preventing high school graduates from booking cruises or in reducing the number of alcohol-related incidents. In 2009, despite having initiated the Age Discrimination legislation, she applied to the Australian Human Rights Commissioner for an exemption from the Act. If granted, this would allow Carnival Australia to prohibit people under the age of 21 from travelling on a cruise ship without an accompanying adult during the yearly schoolies period of 1 November to 30 January. The application was refused, so Carnival Australia appealed the decision.

> *'If I believe something is right or wrong, then I'm prepared to at least have a fight. You don't always win, but I think it's often worth really having robust engagement on those sorts of issues.'*

Ann believed the decision was wrong and told the commission it was impossible to both comply with the Age Discrimination Act and guarantee the safety of passengers on board when there is 'a shipload of kids getting drunk' during schoolies. In the end, Carnival Australia won a temporary exemption from the provision of the Act and was able to implement their 'no schoolies' policy with some adjustments to the conditions.

Fathoming the market

Ann's belief in the importance of flexible thinking and dealing with change was also borne out when she reflects on her transition from a government environment to a commercial one. Ann learned a valuable lesson from mistakes she made in the way she presented her arguments at Westpac. When she first came into the corporate world, she noticed she was unable to connect with some key decision-makers in the bank whenever she spoke the language of government, which focused on policy- and priority-setting, fairness and stakeholder management. For instance, when she first proposed paid maternity leave at Westpac, she ran the argument based on fairness, which would have convinced the public service; however, at the bank, she watched everyone's eyes glaze over as she was talking. She realised that, in order to win over the decision-makers, she had to develop a completely different way of thinking and a different language that would enable her to present a compelling financial argument in a way the bank understood and to which it could respond.

> *'So I went back, girded my loins, shed the tears of frustration — and almost anger, really — but got a different group of people to work with me on the idea, and then came back with the numbers, which were so compelling that we did it.'*

The twists of fate and timing

Ann's entry into Westpac was a fortuitous moment. Bob Joss was hired in 1993 from Wells Fargo in the US to revive the ailing Westpac bank and to modernise and streamline its operations. He was dismayed at the low numbers of senior women at Westpac and instructed the bank to identify female candidates from both public and private sectors for senior roles. Ann was one of those identified.

This was good timing for Ann, who recognised that, with an impending change of government, she needed to take the opportunity presented at Westpac and 'get ahead of the curve' rather than wait for events to control her destiny.

Several years later, while still at Westpac in New Zealand and on a trip back to Australia, Ann was walking down a Sydney street, pondering over what career opportunities might be available, when she ran into the chair of Carnival Australia's Advisory Council, Katie Lahey.

> *'We ran into each other in the street in Sydney and Katie said, "Oh, I've got the perfect job for you," and I went, "Okay." '*

At the time, Carnival Australia's board was grappling with how to rebuild a business with severe reputational damage since the tragic death of Dianne Brimble on a P&O ship in 2002, after she had been drinking and had been given the 'date rape' drug gamma-hydroxybutyrate. Although Ann had no tourism, travel or cruise line experience, Katie knew her to be the perfect person for the job — someone energised by tough challenges, who could face adversity head-on and provide direction in a crisis. Katie convinced a rather traditional board to consider someone from outside the industry. Ann subsequently convinced the US executive that she could turn around the business and was the best person for the job.

Ann has three criteria for assessing a potential change in career. First, an assessment of whether the next job offers something different — some learning, broadening of her experience, and excitement. Secondly, there is the impact on her household; with each opportunity, the big question would always be, 'Will my family come with me?' Ann has now worked in three countries (England, New Zealand and Australia) and shifted across capital cities in Australia seven times, so family considerations had to be high on the agenda with each move. Equally important, however, would be whether the role would enable Ann to make a difference — not just to improve an existing business model, but to dig deeper and recreate the business. So, running Westpac in New Zealand was, on one level, about improving the business. However, on a deeper level, it was about enhancing the reputation of the company and, deeper again, about creating a different look and feel in the market.

'In my current job, the big motivator was to have a crack at something that everybody thought I was completely mad to do.'

Similarly, at Carnival Australia, Ann came in to rebuild the business and restore the reputation of the P&O line. However, the motivation she gets from her work tends to lead her down several paths, and she has since become a passionate advocate for Australian tourism. Ann has also been a force in bringing together a rather disparate and internally competitive tourism sector to engage in debates about presenting a coherent offering from a customer perspective.

Can't do it on your own

The support of Ann's husband, Michael, has been essential. Michael is the person Ann consults most with, probably, as she admits, because he knows her best and gives her wise counsel.

'He knows me well and he's often watched me and said, "Maybe it's time."'

Married at 20, they have since grown up together, learned together, seen the world together and 'fought the good fight' together.[2]

Michael was a highly successful corporate executive at Telstra and, later, at Cricket Australia. As time went on it became increasingly impossible for parallel career paths to run smoothly. If Ann were to relocate to New Zealand to further her career at Westpac, it would have required Michael to give up his job and do something completely different. Needless to say, this decision led to a lot of soul-searching for both of them to resolve how they might work out their career and family challenges.

'It's like — whose turn is it to take the rubbish out, and then changing it halfway through your life.'

Ann admitted that Michael didn't really want to leave the corporate world — he wanted to have things to do and a job. It was a tough choice at a time when it was not common for men to be seen to be giving up their careers because their partner has another job opportunity.

In the event, Michael has been very successful in creating his own consulting business, both when the family moved to New Zealand and again when they relocated back to Sydney. Ann feels he managed to tap into something that he perhaps may not have otherwise tried, and made a great success at it.

Like most successful women, Ann has a strong network of friends who know her well — people she can ring and seek advice from at critical junctures. She has found that people who have known her for a long time give her more honest feedback than others. As her profile and seniority increased she still needed honest feedback but tended to get less of it from people who didn't know her before she was CEO.

'As I've got into more senior roles, people often don't talk to me as honestly as people who knew me before I had any senior roles!'

There's more to life than work

Ann is a passionate advocate of lots of things other than her work and finds equivalent motivation and energy from many areas of her life. Her greatest passions outside work are concerned with making a difference in areas where there is gross unfairness. Ann describes her aim as being to get resources, skills and capabilities to the right people at the right time. Her focus is in two key areas: Indigenous communities, and children and adults with a disability. She has been involved for over 10 years in Jawun, an organisation that seconds corporate executives into Indigenous communities to help the rebuilding process. She is also involved with Indigenous education, raising money to fund scholarships to help Indigenous children finish school and have access to the best education.

Michael and Ann's son, Nick, was born with a disability, and this has undoubtedly been one of the triggers for her engagement and involvement in providing access to sport for children and adults with a disability. Sport is the 'great leveller', as Ann describes it. She has also recently launched the St Vincent de Paul 'Vinnie's CEO Sleep Out 2012', urging CEOs to sleep rough for a night in support of Vinnie's homeless services.

'What I know now'

Ducking and weaving

Looking back, what are the lessons Ann has learned through her career transitions?

The first is learning to be much more adaptable. She describes her younger self as somewhat rigid, stubborn and set in her ways. Once she understood that the outcome is usually more important than the process for reaching it, it was a small step to realising there are lots of different ways to get to that objective. Ann said she needed to learn to work out her objective, and then to become adaptable and flexible when necessary to bring people with her.

Secondly, Ann felt that as she has gotten older she has realised that 'things don't always go your way, even if you think you're right … And being right doesn't always mean you can get there!'

The way to the top

Ann remembers that 20 years ago it seemed there were many aspiring women with an eye on senior roles, and that there were many supportive policies, terms and conditions being developed in the workplace to help them fulfil these roles. There was a level of optimism. However, we know today that, while women may have the skills and capabilities needed for senior appointments, succession plans and policies by themselves are not sufficient to achieve these roles. The problems lie deeper within the organisations.

> 'The new lingo is unconscious bias … I think the problem actually is conscious bias … There's an elephant in the room in Australia that nobody is talking about.'

While she acknowledges the positive work at the board level, Ann believes the key barrier is in the organisational culture. Women are left in support roles, such as legal or human resource appointments, and only a handful of them have been encouraged to move into roles where they have the business accountability essential for getting to the top of an organisation. Women who are at the top of an organisation tend to be there not by coming up through organisations, but by coming in laterally — women like Gail Kelly, for instance, who came to Westpac Australia from sales and marketing roles in other banks, and Sally McDonald, who came into Oroton from consulting. It does make one wonder why the women in these organisations are not coming up through the normal promotional process.

> 'So it's got to be bias; we run out of excuses. There are still tons of women in middle management of organisations, all of whom say they want to stay and they want to progress ... There are women everywhere except at the top of companies.'

What's more, Ann reflects, there are more women at the top of resources and allied industries such as mining than there are in industries like retailing. Possibly this trend is being driven by the rapid rate of growth of these industries and by skill and talent shortages, so that the entrenched conscious bias that is built up over generations in other sectors seems to not take hold in these industries.

The map is not the territory

Ann appears optimistic and perhaps a little pensive around the different reality the place of work holds in the lives of younger women today. She sees younger women testing the world, seeing what's available, trying out a few things first and not being in as much of a hurry as she was when she was building her career.

> 'I always felt, when I was young, I was in a hurry. I had to get to work; I had to finish my degree. I felt that was part of the process of demonstrating you were a proper grown-up ...'

She observes some women completing degrees and then doing something totally different — perhaps working in the not-for-profit sector or applying their professional qualifications in ways that her generation wouldn't have thought about. They are more mobile and are prepared to do completely different things.

Where to next?

The next phase of Ann's life is likely to be unexpected, unplanned and unpredictable, but is sure to capture her energy and enthusiasm.

Ann's successful career is a salutary reminder to all those career coaches and HR practitioners out there who stress the need to plan a career. Perhaps the lesson we can take out of Ann's life is to forget the plan — understand where your passions and energy lie, what you are really good at, and be open to opportunities that will inevitably arise.

Women in Partnership: Yin–Yang Balance

Sarah Rey

Sarah is one of a rare breed of women pioneers who has made a successful move from a comfortable career in a prominent law firm to establish her own firm in 2005.

After serving as Partner at Dunhill Madden Butler and Special Counsel at Blake Dawson, she decided to take the leap into her own private practice, Justitia, along with colleague and close friend Mary-Jane Ierodiaconou. Justitia is now a leading employment, discrimination and OH&S law firm based in Melbourne.

Mary-Jane Ierodiaconou

Mary-Jane is the complementary yin force to Sarah's yang. An accredited mediator and experienced investigator, she is also the financial and reporting brains behind the firm.

Not content with simply leading their own firm, both partners give back to the broader legal community. They are regular speakers at conferences and publish extensively. Sarah is an advisory board member for the Centre of Employment and Labour Relations Law at the University of Melbourne, and a director of the Australian Women's Chamber of Commerce and Industry. Mary-Jane was elected as a Councillor of the Law Institute of Victoria, chaired its Diversity Taskforce, and served on the editorial committee of its multi-award-winning journal.

Pioneering lawyers Sarah Rey and Mary-Jane Ierodiaconou have complementary professional interests, a strong friendship and shared business values, enabling them to build a flourishing and innovative law firm together.

The beginning: a passion for social equality

At university, Sarah and Mary-Jane were passionate about using the law to tackle social inequality. They were both active in the Women's Law Collective — Mary-Jane was involved in a campaign to explain sexual assault laws to year 12 students and worked with migrant and refugee communities, while Sarah was involved in campaigns addressing environmental issues and in student politics.

Law is a broad discipline and there were always going to be many choices after their studies were completed; however, they both entered private practice and worked for a medium-sized firm called Dunhill Madden Butler. There, they were fortunate to have received some positive experiences and mentoring from colleagues in an eclectic environment that tolerated different personalities and interests. This environment meant they were able to survive the notoriously difficult early years, in contrast to many articled clerks at that time, particularly women, who dropped out. Once they were practising solicitors, they both became involved in the longstanding group Feminist Lawyers, consisting of pre-eminent women lawyers working in law firms, government, academia and at the bar, which provided Sarah and Mary-Jane with multiple role models. This inspired Sarah to do voluntary work for Fitzroy Legal Service, and Mary-Jane to volunteer at the Refugee & Immigration Legal Centre.

The importance of family: sowing the seeds

Sarah's and Mary-Jane's families have many similarities. Their mothers were both teachers who taught them the value of a good education, and there was never a sense that education or career was limited by gender. Both their mothers grew up in rural Victoria and left home at an early age as very resourceful young adults. Their fathers, both first-generation migrants, were also extremely supportive of their career choices and could always see the 'big picture'. None of their parents were conventional thinkers; they nurtured in their daughters a strong sense of confidence and the courage to challenge conventional thinking. They also taught Sarah and Mary-Jane about fiscal prudence, so they did not become locked into an expensive lifestyle that restricted their choices in life.

The seed to grow their own business was implanted in each of them from an early age, although perhaps not expressly. Both Sarah and Mary-Jane always understood that working in a corporate law firm required contributing to the running of a profitable business. They always took the initiative for marketing and building client relationships.

As dynamic women lawyers, Sarah and Mary-Jane observed and became frustrated with the culture and practices of traditional, male-dominated big law firms. They came to see that the 'large law firm' model was not working for some of their clients or for themselves. At this point, it became a natural progression for them to pioneer an alternative law practice. What was distinctive about Justitia is that it focused on building a unique and strong partnership, developing exemplary client service, fostering the talent of other women lawyers, and offering an alternative to clients and staff wishing to conduct business in a flexible and harmonious fashion. Since its inception in 2005, Justitia has grown from just Sarah and Mary-Jane to seven lawyers and six legal research assistants.

The state of balance and seamless nature of their partnership is evident early in conversation with Mary-Jane and Sarah. As one begins to talk, thoughts are generated in the other, then bounced back and forth. The women embody an approach to business aligned in every way with their values of transparency and collaboration, and Justitia resonates with positive energy.

Smashing the old paradigm

All law firms are the same. Or are they?

Law firms in Australia tend to be male-dominated, and the trend appears to be shifting in favour of men even more. A survey by *The Australian* in 2010 of the 35 leading law firms found that women accounted for just 21.9 percent of staff promoted to a partnership in the past six months, down from 26.8 percent a year earlier. Half of law graduates are women and by 2013 women solicitors are anticipated to dominate the profession, yet little seems to have changed for the career prospects of women lawyers in 20 years.[1]

Many law firms have a culture that Sarah and Mary-Jane believe holds women back from being innovative or maximising their talents, and which takes a personal toll on the lives of lawyers. Anyone who has worked in large law firms, or is related to a lawyer, or is a client of one of the top-tier law firms, may recognise some of the following:

- A culture that considers the hours and the money as most important, and that money can adequately compensate for anything.

- The drive to push work down the staff hierarchy and encourage clients to speak to less experienced lawyers. Several billable hours could be spent on a task by a first- or second-year solicitor when a senior lawyer could have dealt with it in five minutes, representing poor value for money.

- A hierarchical approach whereby first-year lawyers get the low-level work, and the prospect of challenging work is a carrot for those who stay and complete a tough apprenticeship.

- A focus on the top 10 clients as the key revenue-generators for the firm, to the detriment of supporting smaller clients.

- Highly status-driven cultures in which lawyers are judged according to their position, the fees they earn, billable hours and the clients they manage, with little accommodation for work–life balance.

- The provision of advice that often lacks innovation or creative solutions.

The decision to establish Justitia was based on sound commercial reasoning as much as Mary-Jane's and Sarah's desire to spread their wings and take flight. Both women had been working in large corporate environments for a decade and their feedback from clients indicated the relationships with individual lawyers were valued, but the way services were being delivered was underwhelming. Sarah and Mary-Jane believed it was the underlying culture of law firms that created this dissatisfaction.

Sources of inspiration

Sarah and Mary-Jane have always enjoyed listening to inspirational speakers or reading about the lives of interesting and successful people, and, like many, they also appreciate the stories of success despite adversity or hurdles. However, both are intrigued by the fact that business seems to worship the idea of the single successful hero leader, when in fact many organisations are successful due to a cohesive leadership team at the top. If a leader is successful it is often at the expense of other things in his or her life — for example, health, marriage or children. When they established Justitia, Sarah and Mary-Jane understood that you cannot be all things to all people, and where there was a need for some give on occasion due to work or personal demands, the burden of management needed to be shared. These values shaped their unique and transformational business model.

A transformational business model

'People told us we were crazy, didn't they? Yes, they kept using words like "brave" or "daring", I think some words like that. "Leap of faith".'

Their belief in the importance of client service over billable hours inspired them to set up their own law firm with an alternative culture; there had to be a better way to run a law firm. Sarah and Mary-Jane worked hard to demonstrate that their approach — based, firstly, on delivering services and meeting client needs through teamwork and collaboration; and, secondly, on an assessment of the value of the work delivered to the client, rather than just an account of billable hours — was just as sound a business model.

Justitia works in a collaborative manner with a diverse range of corporate and government clients, advising on the management of staff and all legal and regulatory issues that affect the workplace. These range from the drafting of contracts and policies, enterprise bargaining, performance management and termination of employment, enforcing restraints of trade and protecting intellectual property, Fair Work and the Fair Work Ombudsman, through to equal-opportunity training and assisting clients to manage bullying and other complaints.

The 'clipped-wing syndrome'

'The term that we coined to describe many of our colleagues who had been in those organisations for a very long time without their career progressing, but who did not have the courage to leave, was "clipped-wing syndrome".'

Sarah and Mary-Jane were acutely aware of the 'clipped-wing syndrome'. It afflicted many colleagues in large national firms who were experienced but nevertheless lacked a say in the decision-making: colleagues who were risk-averse, unable to step out and create their own profiles, and who found it difficult to form connections with clients because the business was tightly controlled by the partners. Both women had worked in medium-sized firms where they had experienced greater freedom and collegiality with more seniority, and they were not about to let their wings be clipped.

Nor did they want to clip the wings of their staff. They are very supportive of staff attending all manner of seminars and events that encourage/assist their growth as a successful solicitor and wellbeing as an individual. Mary-Jane and Sarah are relaxed on the subject of hours and offer flexible working arrangements, recognising that an employee with a balanced work–life load who is enjoying work will provide better performance, more satisfied clients and long-term loyalty. To enable this flexibility and accommodate staff working non-standard hours, they expect a high level of communication so everyone can plan their work carefully.

Justitia employs six legal research assistants, law students who work one or two days a week in the practice, learning the gamut of clerical skills as well as conducting legal research. They emerge primed and ready to step into the next stage of their working lives. Sarah and Mary-Jane provide them with information about networking and how to be an effective trainee and solicitor, interviewing tips, and insights into which firm will fit that particular student and vice versa. It is intended to be a very supportive apprenticeship, and the mentoring opportunities within the firm were an unexpected positive aspect of having their own legal practice. The benefit for the firm of reduced secretarial support is self-sufficient lawyers.

What? No billable hour targets?

Justitia's lawyers don't have budgets, nor do they have billable hours as targets. As Mary-Jane posed: 'What's the point of billing a large amount if you don't retain the client relationship?' As lawyers operate in a highly risk-averse environment, some document everything with a 10-page letter and then charge clients for work that may not have been requested. The Justitia approach is to develop a relationship of trust and reliability with clients, and this is done in several ways.

Firstly, there is flexibility in how advice is given, which might be over the telephone or emails. That works very well for Justitia's clients, many of whom are sophisticated and professional human resource managers or corporate counsel who often just need a small matter resolved quickly.

Total collaboration and accessibility is another characteristic of the Justitia–client relationship. When meeting clients for the first time, often both partners go together so clients never have the experience of walls around one person. How seamlessly do they operate? Well, to the extent that both insisted on being interviewed for this book together. Feedback from the clients shows their efforts to provide a complete and broad 'whole firm' relationship is appreciated, although it has confused the occasional client who rings to ask for Sarah-Jane!

They practice accessibility and openness around fees as well, and are absolutely committed to being transparent on this matter. There's no such thing as a lump-sum fee — all invoices are itemised.

Justitia prides itself on innovation. During the global financial crisis, they understood that their clients were particularly cost-conscious and in need of certainty. To assist with this, they developed a range of products such as policies and template contracts, an unusual practice for law firms. Justitia also runs regular training programs and a dedicated training website. This responsiveness is part of their commitment to empowering clients and avoiding the creation of one-way dependent relationships.

Turning points

> 'So we were prepared to give it a go, and if it were to fail then we had many other options to pursue … at the end of the day, you just have to say, "What have I got to lose? Nothing. We're highly employable and we've got everything to gain." '

A key turning point for Justitia arrived when it dawned on Sarah and Mary-Jane that the practice was going to be bigger than the two of them and they decided to employ their first lawyer. Each subsequent hiring decision was a major step because of their commitment to giving staff the opportunity to perform and grow. They once had to make the decision to let a staff member go after a short period and they described the conversation as excruciating. They have since developed empathy for clients who face these kinds of conversations on a regular basis.

Each decision concerning office space was significant, too. The practice began in the front room of Sarah's house, but when Mary-Jane joined they quickly realised they would need more space and took a lease on Queen Street. Two years later they moved to a larger office on William Street, and another three years later to bigger premises again.

One important decision was to only work at an organisational level. The practice was receiving frequent individual referrals from colleagues, but after two years they had the confidence to say that this was not what the business was about. Their decision was made to uphold the commitment to client relationships that were long-term and provide total service — something that could only happen with organisations that had ongoing and multiple legal requirements.

An appointment to the panel of a major bank in 2006 was another big step. They were recognised by both *The Financial Review* and colleagues as 'punching above their weight'. However, six years later they are still on the panel.

Key lessons: honesty, prudence and patience

Throughout their partnership, Sarah and Mary-Jane have honed their business skills so that they run the business in a sustainable manner, keeping all stakeholders happy.

They have learnt not to outsource the financial aspects of the business to anyone but rather to control these entirely themselves. They have also learnt that, when they make a mistake, they need to be completely upfront with the client about it and make amends in a way that is satisfactory to the client.

As a small firm, they have learnt not to bite off more than they can chew from a financial point of view. It pays to be patient and take an organic approach rather than financially overextending by recruiting staff, engaging expensive consultants or leasing opulent premises. The assessment of the return on the investment is a critical one for any business, but particularly for small ones.

Yin–yang

'We both have husbands but we refer to the Justitia partnership as our second marriage.'

Mary-Jane and Sarah both acknowledge that there have been working periods involving long hours and they have often wondered if they had to grow as fast as they did.

Having two heads has been useful in managing the challenges and stresses of keeping a business afloat, as not every lawyer and not every business person is good at all the diverse aspects of running a business. They recognise that both are good at most of the tasks, so dividing up the work is as much a question of predilections as of abilities. Mary-Jane shows a preference for finance and reporting systems management, while Sarah turns to the marketing and building the clientele of the practice. They see themselves as businesswomen and lawyers in tandem, relishing the management, marketing and day-to-day practical realities of running a business, as well as the legal work. And when one is overloaded, the other can spot the signs and step in with some help, or even just a cup of tea.

Communication is key to their successful business relationship with each other. The pair believes in the constructive power of disagreements and they have clearly worked out a way to listen to each other, recognising that if one has a burning desire to do something then it must be for a good reason. Likewise, on recruiting decisions, if one has a reservation about an applicant then the process does not proceed. Problems are shared and they talk to each other daily, even if not in the office. When one is on holiday, the partner remaining in the office keeps a running diary of the daily events.

They share values on life outside work as well, and that has sustained them. Avoiding burnout has been critical, and to avoid this they support each other's efforts to maintain external interests. Keeping fit and healthy is important for both, as is having a sabbatical arrangement in place whereby they take a couple of months off every five years.

Defining success

To Sarah and Mary-Jane, success in career terms is about meeting their personal goals while remaining true to their values. These values include contributing more widely to society. It is one of the reasons that the pro bono practice is important to Justitia and they value their relationships with the not-for-profit sector. Success in the legal profession is also about sustainable lawyering and mentoring of colleagues. It is a marathon, not a race.

Their legacy will be to build a firm that is a role model within the legal profession: a firm that is a successful practice, acting for diverse organisations while working in a sustainable manner. This includes embracing flexible work practices so that staff and partners can continue working as lawyers over the whole of their working lives.

What's next

'I think when you're a smaller size like us you can be nimble in your decision-making and you can make decisions very quickly. We don't need to consult 10 committees and that also fosters innovation.'

The pair is often asked how big they want to grow the business. They acknowledge that the next step of taking on more partners would be a major one. Their firm embraces innovation as a key to growth. It recently adopted a social media strategy to share its intellectual property more broadly and, consequently, the firm's website is regularly used by clients and the media to keep updated on the latest developments in workplace law. In late 2012, the firm was appointed to the Commonwealth Government's legal panel — a significant step, as it entails a commitment to advising agencies throughout Australia.

Clearly some major decisions are to come for Mary-Jane and Sarah in terms of where they take the practice next. Whatever transpires, they will certainly be made in accordance with the sound values that have made the firm such an outstanding leader for lawyers who want to crack the mould.

Theresa Gattung
Cracking the Glass Ceiling

Theresa Gattung has been named in *Fortune* magazine's list of the 50 most powerful women in international business several times since 2002. In 2006, she was named in *Forbes*'s list of the world's most powerful women across any sphere.

Major Turning Points

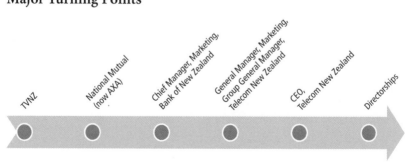

TVNZ

National Mutual (now AXA)

Chief Manager, Marketing, Bank of New Zealand

General Manager, Marketing, Group General Manager, Telecom New Zealand

CEO, Telecom New Zealand

Directorships

The word *passion* takes on a whole new meaning when you talk with Theresa Gattung, and there are few people with such burning ambition and confidence. One cannot help but be caught up in her energy and enthusiasm for her causes — from running New Zealand Telecom, to her love of horses and her mission to create a new world-class animal care centre with Wellington's Society for the Prevention of Cruelty to Animals (SPCA).

'Chief girl'

'Because I was the eldest, I think I was quite bossy.'

Theresa is a straight-talker and describes herself as somewhat assertive in her younger years and as someone who always intended to succeed. Growing up, she loved reading and debating and planned to become a 'crusading lawyer of some type'. At the same time, she was fascinated by business and chose to study a management degree. While at university she read a motivational and inspiring book about women in management in New Zealand by Helen Place[1] and decided she would become a chief executive officer of a large company in New Zealand by the time she was 40. No-one told her she couldn't, so why not? It took nearly 20 years for Theresa to realise this goal and be crowned queen of New Zealand's largest publicly listed company at the age of 37.

Theresa credits her family upbringing as a key influence in her drive and determination to succeed. She describes both her parents as adventurous, entrepreneurial and resourceful; they were first-generation immigrants from Britain who came to New Zealand in search of a better life for their family. Both established their own businesses: her father in commercial property, and her mother made products for the tourist market.

She was the eldest in an all-girl family, and had a father who did not see any barriers to female success. Her parents, and her upbringing, had a powerful effect on the young Theresa, who wrote in her autobiography of telling her grandparents she was 'chief girl'.[2] She was 17 before she first experienced gender discrimination; her male teachers thought girls couldn't do maths as well as the boys could. But by then it was too late to affect her.

> 'You know what 17-year-olds are like ... they think they know everything. So it had no impact on me. My self-esteem, my view that I could do anything and that I was quite brainy, was already formed.'

On a mission

Some of Theresa's career turning points were serendipitous; others were opportunistic, and others still were well planned. However, all were based on the pursuit of her ultimate goal: to reach a prime position of power and authority in the business/corporate world.

When Theresa finished her business degree, she decided to simultaneously take up a law degree and to find a job that would utilise her business degree. She approached TVNZ (TV New Zealand) when studying law and was employed as Market Research Officer in Sales and Marketing. She loved the organisation and the work so much that she stayed there. But her urge for studying and practising law was still there, so she decided to complete her law degree while still working full-time at TVNZ. She recalls she had a very supportive manager at the time. However, while studying law in Wellington she decided that there were few roles for crusading lawyer types, and that she was not well suited to being a lawyer. The first turning point in her career therefore came when she realised her somewhat romantic, Hollywood notion of what a lawyer did was unrealistic, and she was able to let go of this fantasy and continue her commercially focused business career. Not that her law degree was in any way wasted — it has been an invaluable touchstone throughout her business career, particularly in commercial decision-making.

She did extraordinarily well and soon moved through the ranks. While she loved the experience of managing people and running significant marketing events, boredom set in after a few years and Theresa decided it was time to move on. By this time her focus was on becoming an investment banker, but to no avail.

'I think that I'd watched too many TV programs. I couldn't get in, the investment banking sector was overtly sexist.'

Nevertheless, the next move was into the financial services industry with National Mutual (now AXA) as Marketing Research Manager. When she attended a global talent-development program run by National Mutual and was the only woman there, she realised she was never going to reach her goals in this male-oriented organisation and began looking for another opportunity.

The Bank of New Zealand (BNZ) advertised for a head of marketing, so Theresa applied and was successful, starting work at the beginning of what proved to be a very tumultuous time in the bank's history. After floating on the share market in 1987, by 1989 the bank almost reached a state of collapse. In June 1989, BNZ announced a $648 million loss driven principally by the investment banking group's exposure to property and investment risk. The announcement spurred the government into action and it organised a private sector–dominated recapitalisation of the BNZ worth $610 million. Despite the new National government injecting $200 million directly into the BNZ the following year, in late 1990 the bank announced further losses loss of $71 million and the government finally decided to sell the BNZ. The National Australia Bank (NAB) bought the bank for $1.48 billion.[3]

Theresa credits working in the bank during this tumultuous time as an enormous learning curve in her business career. However, after the acquisition by NAB, she felt that her autonomy had eroded and that BNZ seemed to be relegated to Australian subsidiary branch status rather than a fully-fledged, independent national enterprise. It was time to move on, so Theresa set her sights on pursuing her CEO dream elsewhere.

'Question: When is the best time for your car to break down?

Answer: when a passing motorist who helps you just happens to be the head of marketing at Telecom, and is about to be leaving his job.'

One day after having a driving incident, she flagged down a passing motorist who just happened to be the head of marketing at Telecom. Theresa took the opportunity to take him to lunch to thank him for helping her out, when she learned that he was leaving to return to the US shortly. Theresa decided that this had to be her next job. In undertaking her research, she read that the search firm engaged in finding a replacement had concluded there were no New Zealanders suitable for the role. Naturally, she decided to take matters into her own hands and called the CEO of Telecom directly. After the usual round of interviews and reference-checking, she was offered the role.

A dream come true

Theresa had had her sights on the CEO role from her first day at Telecom and took five years to achieve it. She joined as General

Manager of Marketing in September 1994 and was promoted in 1996 to run the whole New Zealand business. Throughout her time at Telecom, Theresa had put substantial resources into cultivating relationships and networks, both internally and with influential external stakeholders. She then seized the moment in 1999, when Sir Roderick Deane announced his intention to take up the Chair role. Theresa describes going into 'Project CEO Mode', which included intensive interview skills practice and a wardrobe makeover.

On 12 August 1999, Telecom announced that Theresa would become the Chief Executive Officer.

> *'This was my dream come true, the moment I had worked towards for nearly 20 years since I had sat in my room in Hamilton, reading Helen Place's book and setting my goal. I had been brought up to believe that anything was possible and now, at the age of 37, with a couple of years to spare, I had proved it.'*

Theresa was the first woman to run a publically listed New Zealand company, and she held this position for eight challenging years. During this period, she steered the company through a period of substantial change in the business and regulatory environment and became embroiled in a major political agenda around re-regulation of the industry.

Despite the uniqueness of her position and the challenges of the time, commendations of her work flowed in: in 2002, *The Independent* reported that Telecom NZ was probably the top-performing company worldwide in its sector for the half year to December;[4] in June 2002, London consultants IR Group named Telecom NZ the world's best performer in the global telecommunications sector;[5] in August 2006, *Forbes* magazine ranked Theresa the 49th most influential woman in the world;[6] and Boston Consulting Group declared Telecom New Zealand the second-biggest creator of value for shareholders in New Zealand (after Fletcher Building) in the five years to the end of 2007,[7] the year Theresa left the company.

Problems — you're standing in it

Yet these high points were also peppered with considerable lows: in May 2006, Telecom NZ was made aware, by the biggest leak of a government document in modern New Zealand political history, of the government's intention to heavily regulate the telecommunications industry and pursue an aggressive strategy of unbundling (separation of the retail and network businesses). Consequently, the company suffered a $3.3 billion drop in share-market value. Theresa was heavily criticised by the media and by angry fund managers for not managing the situation better. With *The New Zealand Herald* publishing a barrage of critical articles about her during this time, the spotlight was on Theresa almost daily!

Why such a backlash when the debate around unbundling and regulation had been argued backwards and forwards in New Zealand since 2000? According to Theresa, the backlash was created by the shock and surprise of the government's reversal of its position on unbundling from just the previous year, which caught the market totally unprepared.

Out in the wilderness

Theresa remembers the press treatment of this story over the several months that followed as a 'David and Goliath' one, with Telecom as the Goliath. It was a tremendously stressful period of vilification and unfair accusations, while Theresa still had to manage the company and her team. She was exhausted, distressed about what was happening, uncertain about what to do next, and felt very alone. Perhaps *execution* is too strong a word, but for Theresa it felt like a drawn-out public beheading.

At this point, Theresa's career success also came at a severe personal cost — her 22-year relationship with John Savage came to an end just before the major events unfolded at Telecom. After a protracted period of trying to make the relationship work, Theresa and John parted ways, although they remain friends. Theresa speaks of the difficulty of leading a balanced life as the head of a company, working long hours and travelling a lot, especially as a 'full-on' person. She admits she didn't give much thought to the impact of this on her relationship.

'There were three of us in the marriage, alright: me, him and my job.'

Getting back on the horse

'I believe that things always work out for the best in the end. So, if they haven't worked out for the best, it's not yet the end.'

Theresa's life is very different now and, while she occasionally misses her old life, she can see there are many different ways to live — not one that involves always living on the edge. Instead, she has constructed a life for herself that is flexible, where she can be completely responsible only to herself and not have to 'wear the institution on [her] forehead'.

'I look at those experiences and I say I'm a much better person for having gone through those years, but that was a very difficult time. If I was coming up to it and I was in my 30s and could have avoided it, I absolutely would have done.'

Theresa took a year off after leaving Telecom to get herself back together again physically and emotionally. She used the time to ride her beloved horses, swim every day, travel extensively and spend time with people she loves in places she loves. In 2009, she wrote of her experiences in *Bird on a Wire* (published by Random House).

By the end of that period, she felt able to seriously look at what she loved doing and what she was passionate about but had never had the time for. The answers came quite readily: she loved animals and taking on causes, so she accepted an opportunity with the Wellington SPCA, turning around a distressed organisation that had no government funding and needed strong commercial acumen. Two immediate challenges for the board were selecting a new CEO and creating a new world-class animal care centre at the historic Fever Hospital site.

Theresa was also Chair of the New Zealand Advisory Group for the Frankfurt Book Fair 2012, and is involved with a number of not-for-profit and philanthropic interests, including being co-founder and trustee of the Eva Doucas Charitable Trust and Chair of the Wellington SPCA.

Her personal and not-for-profit interests are balanced with strong commercial and financial directorships. From July 2008 to March 2011, Theresa was Chair of Wool Partners International. In this role, she led the company's drive to reinvigorate the international market for New Zealand's strong wools. Theresa joined the AIA Australia board as an Independent Director in May 2009 and was appointed Chair of the Board in March 2010, and this directorship leverages her insurance and financial services background. In 2012, AIA Australia was awarded the *Financial Review* Smart Investor Blue Ribbon Life Company of the Year.

To add to this impressive list of commitments, Theresa also spends large period of time in public speaking, coaching and mentoring around the world, largely regarding women in leadership and developing women's careers.

However, the portfolio of directorships she holds today came slowly. One of her regrets is that she did not prepare very well for an eventual transition out of Telecom. She had several opportunities to take up directorships while there, which she did not pursue ('too busy and waiting for the perfect one'). When the end came in the unforeseen way that it did, she was not well positioned. Not surprisingly, during her time in the wilderness, offers for her to take up board positions were hardly forthcoming. More than one board considered her too hot to handle.

Perhaps her mixture of commercial and personal interests reflects who she is now as much as any career transitions she's made. They reflect her passions and interests, where she likes to spend her time, and whom she likes to spend it with.

Can't do it on your own

Over the years, Theresa has kept files of press clippings and articles on successful women she has admired. They include Dr Sharon Lord, a former US Deputy Assistant Secretary of Defence, whom she met aboard an America's Cup supporter's boat in 1992. Never one to let an opportunity pass, Theresa introduced herself, only to find out that Sharon was about to move to New Zealand with her husband, Tom Burns, Roderick Deane's predecessor as the CEO of Telecom. Sharon, after relocating to New Zealand, became Theresa's mentor throughout her BNZ years and early Telecom years, and Theresa credits her with helping her navigate the pathway from middle to senior management.

Roderick Deane's support and mentorship also became instrumental in Theresa's rise to the top of Telecom New Zealand:

'I think every generation has a few men who actually really, really get it and sometimes they have more success than others influencing their peers. Roderick was definitely one of those.'

One of her core confidantes during the Telecom crisis was Kevin Roberts, CEO of Saatchi & Saatchi, whom she met during her time at BNZ. She describes Kevin as one of the smartest and most visionary people she has ever dealt with, and she sought his advice at a time when she needed an outside perspective on how to think about shareholders, customers and staff interactions and dynamics.

How do you be a woman in a man's world?

'I switched off my "feminine" side years ago in order to get to the top in a man's world, and then I found some difficulty in switching it on again.'

Throughout her career, Theresa wrestled with how she could tackle the male-dominated environment of the corporate world while remaining true to her own identity. She describes herself as naturally a very team-oriented person; cultivating talent was a passion, and she was always good at choosing the best team then adding her own magic to the mix. It's a testament to her ability to develop capability in her executive team that many of the people who worked for Theresa through the BNZ and Telecom years have gone on to become CEOs of major companies as well as great, long-term friends.

Yet she believes the transactional nature of the corporate

business world demands a tough public persona. Theresa believes women are more exposed to criticism for being too tough than a man who may be considered as strong in the same situation. 'I believe it is still harder for women to get to the top than it is for men,' she writes in *Bird on a Wire*. 'It's harder to become CEO and to be seen as a leader. I think the image of a CEO is still one of a hard-driving male … I don't think the criteria for being a CEO is different for men or women. I do, however, think the margins of error are smaller for women in leadership positions.'[8] While she has seen more women take on senior roles over the last decade or so, and believes it is easier for women in corporate Australia than when she started her career, she still observes the stridency of criticism levelled at women in power, such as Julia Gillard (Australia's first female prime minister), which is at least partly gender-related.

As Theresa sees it, a balance of male and female energy is one of the most important success factors for leaders today. Too much male energy leads to thinking in silo, whereas too much female energy leads to a lack of focus. Role models who exemplify the gift of balance? Well, they include Hilary Clinton, who has redefined her image into one that is softer and more positive (and whom Theresa has met); and Christine Lagarde, Managing Director of the International Monetary Fund, who, according to Theresa, exemplifies a combination of intellect and graciousness (and whom she would love to meet).

'What I know now': lessons for her younger self

Imagine you were able to go back in time and give your younger, 20-year-old self some advice. What might it be? For Theresa, there are three big pieces of advice she'd give her 20-year-old self.

Firstly, there's no need to be in such a hurry — life is a marathon, not a sprint. Take career advancement in your stride and concentrate on performing well.

Secondly, you will never know everything you need to know about a situation. You need to have goals, but also to understand that things happen that you just can't control. The way her role ended at Telecom was an example of a time that she didn't, and couldn't, foresee. She had been discussing her move out of Telecom for some time with Roderick — but on her terms. In her 20s and 30s, Theresa thought she could at least influence, if not control, most outcomes. She now no longer believes that, and understands more about when to steer and when to allow events to happen.

Finally, listen to that quiet voice inside you — the one that alerts you when something doesn't feel right. The one you need to answer to when you reflect on the impact of your decisions. When Theresa first became CEO at Telecom NZ, she committed herself to listening to that small voice, but the frenetic pace, lack of sleep and pressure to make quick decisions can drown it out. Take time to create a little bubble of space so your quiet voice can be heard, whether it be about children, your job, or other things.

More generally, as a woman in corporate life, there are still barriers to and issues regarding getting to the top. So carefully select the company you work for, the boss you work for, the partner you choose, how many children you have — and ensure you work in a part of the business that is crucial and strategic to that company. Be accountable for something related to the bottom line or for delivering a major project. Put yourself in a situation where your contribution is measurable, otherwise you'll be sidelined and may be the first to go when times get tough.

'If you want to be a CEO, you must get into line management

jobs as soon as you can, to get sufficient experience and cover the bases.'

Where to next?

Having achieved a CEO position at 37 years of age, what is next for a driven woman who has only just turned 50? She hasn't ruled out going back to a CEO role, but she is quite relaxed about not knowing where her life will take her. Perhaps she is taking some of the advice she would give her younger self. She started her career wanting to be a crusading lawyer and then rejecting it, but is still passionate about following causes and interests that inspire her. Some might say she has turned her career into a heroic mission and narrowly avoided a beheading.

I suspect we haven't heard the last of Theresa Gattung.

Terri Janke
Driven by a Vision

Terri Janke is an Indigenous arts lawyer with a passion for asserting Indigenous people's rights to their cultural and intellectual property. Terri has represented many Indigenous musicians, writers, language centres, filmmakers, artists, and others across various fields of the arts and culture. And she loves to write, sing and dance herself.

She has drafted and formulated special provisions in complex commercial documentation to cover cultural protocols for Indigenous peoples. Terri has also worked as the Program Officer at the Aboriginal and Torres Strait Islander Arts Unit of the Australia Council, where she was responsible for administering programs for Indigenous music, dance and drama.

Terri writes and lectures extensively in issues relating to Indigenous cultural and intellectual property rights.

Major Turning Points

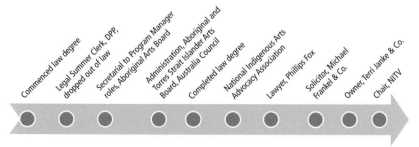

Commenced law degree

Legal Summer Clerk, DPP, dropped out of law

Secretarial to Program Manager roles, Aboriginal Arts Board

Administration, Aboriginal and Torres Strait Islander Arts Board, Australia Council

Completed law degree

National Indigenous Arts Advocacy Association

Lawyer, Phillips Fox

Solicitor, Michael Frankel & Co.

Owner, Terri Janke & Co.

Chair, NITV

'I'm very proud of this'

Terri's parents were a couple blessed with the ability and desire to create a life that would upend their own limiting circumstances and open opportunities for their three children. Her mother, Joanna, grew up in other relations' homes after both her parents died before she was 10. She commenced nursing after her schooling, but eventually pursued a career in government. Her father, John, grew up in a small town in Queensland and worked as a Postmaster-General's Department employee from telegram boy to postman before becoming a postal officer. In 1972 to 1975, John worked as a law clerk for the Australian Legal Aid Office, studying communications part-time.

Although both her parents did not further their formal education beyond years eight and 10, they were both clearly intelligent people. Her father read as much as he possibly could and wrote articles for various publications. It was her father's passion to become a journalist that led to the family moving to Canberra. With books at home, their parents' nurturing and encouragement to do well at school, and their recognition that life did not have to be limiting, it was inevitable that Terri and her siblings would at least get to university and pursue meaningful careers.

Terri was nine years old when the family moved from Cairns to Canberra. Racism was endemic in Cairns in the 1970s, and Terri remembers losing friends because she was Indigenous and so was stereotyped as a kid who would never do well at school. To make matters worse, Terri was a skinny kid who constantly had a runny nose and suffered badly from eczema, which would make her skin very itchy and weepy. Moving out of this limiting and racist environment and also to a cooler climate was a positive move for her and also for her brother and sister. Terri believes her parents made the decision to move because they thought 'it was good for them, their own careers and their own personal goals, but I really think they thought of us as well'. Yet moving to Canberra was somewhat of a double-edged sword. Her parents were young — in their 30s — and relocating meant leaving behind a supportive extended family of aunties, uncles and cousins to move to a city where they knew no-one. Eventually, they reconnected with other Aboriginal and Torres Strait Islander people who came from different parts of Australia to work in Canberra.

'That first patch of racism when you're really small has a silencing effect.'

Terri remembers Canberra as being culturally diverse. While they were the only Indigenous Australian children at their Catholic school, there were other non-white children such as Africans and Asians. However, there were still times in Canberra that she was singled out. One of Terri's vivid memories was running down the hill as fast as she could to get home after school, having been bullied, followed, called derogatory names and had rocks thrown at her. Her older, physically stronger sister, Toni, who was also lighter-skinned than Terri, dealt with the abuse by standing up for herself and for Terri. She would be the one running after them or the one to swear at them. Terri, on the other hand, did not want to attract attention to herself; she preferred to 'fly under the radar' and noticed other migrant friends of hers feeling the same way. However, this desire to hide her difference didn't last. By the time she was around 16 years of age, she remembers deciding, 'I'm not going to hide it anymore.' The racism became a motivating force for Terri to 'just get on with it'.

'It was probably around 16 when I thought, "This is absolutely ridiculous," and I thought, "I'm very proud of this [being Indigenous]," and I just wanted to read and follow up and be inspired by people that my parents are bringing to the house and get involved with the work that they were doing, and do more reading and go and see films.'

Drifting into law — why not, so what?

'I'd gone to law school because it was something that, as an Indigenous person, you can help Indigenous people's social justice causes. Or your sister's doing it, and your mum and dad think how great it would be to have a lawyer in the family. You're doing it for everyone else.'

Upon finishing school Terri admits that she didn't think very deeply about enrolling in her arts/law degree at the University of New South Wales. She had considered studying journalism, having always loved reading and writing, but her parents thought it would be good if she stayed with her older sister — they were close, her sister had a great deal of influence over Terri, and Terri was happy to follow what she was doing, so they went to Sydney together to study law. Paradoxically, although her sister's decision to study law influenced Terri to do the same, her sister soon found she didn't like law and never practised. However, unlike Terri, she did finish her law degree the first time round.

Terri, on the other hand, took two attempts with a four-year break in between to complete hers. She began law school with a romantic, Hollywood idea of fighting for social justice in the courts, influenced by the protagonists in *To Kill a Mockingbird* or the television program *L.A. Law*. She would do battle in cases of injustice where there were clear boundaries between winners and losers, right and wrong, good and bad. So she was quite happy to work with the Commonwealth Director of Public Prosecutions during her second-year summer clerkship — until reality struck and she learned there is not always a clear winner or loser, and that access to the legal system is not available to everybody. She didn't like the nature of the work in the courts and she dropped out of law school.

Terri worked with the Aboriginal Arts Board (now the Aboriginal and Torres Strait Islander Arts Board), within the Australia Council, for about four years, starting with secretarial roles and then holding program manager positions. She learned about copyright law (something that wasn't normally covered in law school until fourth year) and related legal issues for Indigenous artists, such as the problems they had in making their works available and with contracts. At the time, she was very happy to work for the Aboriginal community, to remain in a government role at the Aboriginal Arts Board, and to prevaricate about completing her law degree.

At the Aboriginal Arts Board, Terri worked for a young 30-something manager, Lesley Fogarty. Lesley was a very passionate woman and driven with a very systematic approach to work. Terri credits Lesley with helping her understand that success comes through just that kind of focus and effort, and also with teaching her to be strong on administration and process. 'I guess government can do that for you,' says Terri. 'It's the only bureaucratic job I've had.' But these skills were also to serve Terri well outside government, when she later developed a career in intellectual and copyright law.

Lesley was very supportive of Terri's development while they were working together, although she had high standards. Lesley supported Terri's ideas, provided opportunities for her to become involved in particular projects, provided her with positive feedback and helped her advance through the government bureaucracy quickly. She also encouraged Terri to stop being a fence-sitter, and to make a decision about whether to do her law degree once and for all or to drop the idea.

Finding her passion

'I never focused on wanting to do something as much as this, when I finally worked it all out.'

While working at the Aboriginal Arts Board, Terri had become fascinated with copyright issues, seeing firsthand the problems faced by Aboriginal and Torres Strait Islander artists in making their works available. This exposure defined her subject choice and her search for voluntary or part-time work until her degree was finished.

What convinced her was the thought that 'Here's an accessible area of law for Indigenous people. It not about them always having to be the defendant, but they are the applicant, and asserting their rights to their art work, or their rights to their knowledge.' This was a positive place for Aboriginal people, and she wanted to be part of it.

She worked part-time at a law firm and volunteered at a legal centre and with the National Indigenous Arts Advocacy Association (NIAAA). It was here that Terri's interest in Indigenous cultural and intellectual property was consolidated towards the end of her law degree. She worked with three creative, encouraging and inspiring people. The first was Colin Golvan, a barrister in intellectual property and who was working on a famous copyright case, *Milpurrurru v Indofurn*,[1] at the time. Colin allowed Terri to be involved in some of the discussions so that she would get an understanding of this area of law. The two other inspirational people were lawyer Michael McMahon, who was Director of the NIAAA at the time; and the Chair of the association, Bronwyn Bancroft, an Indigenous artist. Bronwyn was a strong role model who offered encouragement and support for Terri's early career as an arts lawyer.

Terri became captivated by every aspect of copyright. She was interested in changing the law, knowing the law, analysing every aspect of why it didn't fit in with Indigenous cultural interests, and looking at how that system might be adapted, or improved for Indigenous rights. She discovered her 'calling' as a way of helping people out and making a difference, utilising both her legal knowledge and her talent in connecting with people through her own love of the arts world. She was a singer, a performer and a writer, and so could readily connect with people in artistic ways. Terri said she would have worked for nothing, and in fact she did a substantial amount of voluntary and pro bono work both during her degree and since then.

After graduating, Terri became a solicitor at Michael Frankel's boutique law firm, Michael Frankel & Company. In 1999, Michael put her in charge of a study into Indigenous cultural and intellectual property, resulting in *Our Culture: Our Future — Report on Australian Indigenous Cultural and Intellectual Property Rights*, which contained 115 legislative and policy recommendations. Legal change was a long time coming, but her report stood the test of time and is still used to inform Indigenous policy to today. This was a turning point in her career.

Going out on her own

Terri did decide to complete her law degree, and found it was a completely different experience the second time round. Maybe she was older and more mature, but with her experience at the Aboriginal Arts Board behind her she was a lot more focused so that 'every subject I did I angled into the career I was going to have'.

Establishing her own practice was a big shift for Terri. She had never thought that she would own a law firm. She says she still can't believe it.

Reflecting back on this time, Terri's decision to establish her own practice was grounded on four key factors that seemed to coalesce in an opportune way.

First, the guidance of her husband, Andrew, was probably the most significant thing that helped Terri beyond anything else and was the foundation for her success. Terri and Andrew met at university. They always got on well and discussed their ambitions and goals, and as these merged together they forged a positive and strong relationship, supporting each other through life. 'I guess love can do that for you,' says Terri. 'He gives up a lot of his time, and I am grateful.' Terri learned a lot about business from her husband, who was not only a great ideas man and a doer, but also the strong emotional support Terri needed to make the decision to set up in business.

Secondly, and just as importantly, their children, Tamina and Jaiki, are also somehow connected to the decision to go out in business. After Jaiki was born, Terri's attention began to shift towards creating a long-term focus in her life. She wanted a goal that would keep her motivated for the next 40 years or so of her working life. She reflected on what her legacy might be, how she could remain relevant, and the things she would like to be proud of. Her decision to set up her own practice would enable her to create a flexible lifestyle that accommodated a family.

> 'There was a shift in my thinking that I could be not just an employed solicitor, but someone who could do much more. The shift there was about saying, "I want to look at what it would be in 40 years, 50 years, 60 years. What impact would I have?"'

Thirdly, Terri had developed some long-term goals, and wanted to have some choice and control over her work and her client base. She also wanted the freedom to be able to offer as much or as little pro bono work as she thought necessary for her clients without the constraints of seeking permission from an employer. These goals would be best achieved working for herself in her own business.

Finally, Terri had developed the confidence to go out on her own. One of the big lessons Terri learned while working with Michael Frankel was his ability to be a passionate lawyer with a heart, but also to run a successful business. She had developed a critical level of confidence after the success of leading *Our Culture: Our Future* and was emotionally ready to establish her own practice.

Transcending childhood

> 'In year 11, we had an English class and the teacher, Mrs Pacey, she said, "Okay, we're all going to keep journals," as part of it, so you just write whatever comes into your head, or stuff like that. I really loved that, and I've kept a journal ever since then. I have lots of them.'

Terri also had an ambition to write novels and did a lot of writing in the first five years of her law practice, when the children were quite young. Her writing is an addition, rather than a transition, to her career.

Terri has always loved writing and words. Her father was an avid reader and a journalist, and she remembers running home after school and burying herself in a book. She particularly loved creative writing and was moved by the wordplay and use of literature, even poetry, as much as a storyline. She has kept a journal since her year 11 English teacher suggested it, and she uses this as a source of ideas for short stories that may someday be useful for a larger piece of work. When she wrote her first novel, *Butterfly Song*,[2] she drew on the journal. Terri finds the process of writing really enabled her to develop insights into herself and a lot of the things that were holding her back. Writing the book was somewhat like taking a burden off her shoulders. She remembers thinking, 'Oh, this is a weight off my shoulders. Thank God it's gone.'

Writing *Butterfly Song* made Terri realise she was probably very affected by racism as a child — in her experience, when you're a kid you're never ready for the discrimination, and so when it happens you don't know how to react. The effects can be as small or as large as the way you hold yourself in the world to avoid being called names. Before writing the book, she had not reflected on how those experiences might have impacted the way she projected herself or how she made career choices.

Although Terri's family grew up in a time that was not as racially unfavourable as previous Aboriginal and Torres Strait Islander generations had endured, they had their own problems. 'We had the legacy of a lot of really bad government practices. I grew up in a town in Far North Queensland, where people's judgments were based on skin colour, how smart someone was, how clean they kept themselves, whether they could rent a house, or even get served in a shop. As my mother Joanna would reflect on her experience, "The banks would not even consider lending you money unless you gave them your soul."'

But Terri now considers that the worst thing is to let these experiences hold you back. The book is a positive one and she used fiction to look at the situation in the 1970s and show that things are different in the 2000s. 'I learned that you can transcend it … and that's the metaphor in the title … I think that I had let [my experiences] limit me, but we're talking about childhood wounds that you carry with you.'

Terri has also written a book with each of her children: *What Makes a Tree Smile*, with Tamina Pitt, and *Kin Island*, with Jaiki Pitt.

A balancing act

'I just won't let go of writing; I can't. I still can't let it go. I want to write.'

Terri seems to be torn between being a writer and a lawyer — she is finding it very challenging to be both — as well as a mother and a wife. She reflects on points in her life when she really wants to write or spend a lot of time writing, but for the moment the law always wins. Particularly as *Butterfly Song* was a cathartic experience, 'After I wrote the book I didn't really feel so driven to keep writing … it was strengthening in terms of my own personal development.' She still does a lot of writing but not with the intention of publishing; however, she doesn't discount more of that in the future. 'I can come back to writing maybe when my children are older.'

Right now, her practice is growing. She's enjoying developing her management skills, and with her children more independent she has an opportunity to focus on developing the business. Part of her 10-year vision, beyond her own business, is to see more Indigenous people working in the law using her own experience a model that others could build on. She has not taken the more common government route and has been running a successful law firm for 12 years. She's still passionate about protecting intellectual property rights for Indigenous artists and has pushed for change for many years now.

Dealing with disappointment

> '... one particular disappointment always sets you up for the next thing that might turn good.'

Terri feels she has not had any significant disappointments in her life or career to date, and is somewhat philosophical about not reflecting too much on disappointments. Nevertheless, she firmly believes that learning from disappointments or failures can help achieve success with future matters. For example, *Our Culture: Our Future* was released just prior to a change of government, so very little change occurred in the area of Indigenous intellectual property for 12 years after the recommendations were published — and dwelling on these disappointments could hold her back if she let them. She would rather recognise there are some things she can't control but she can still keep pushing towards the ultimate goal of a change in Indigenous IP recognition.

Terri also believes in having a perspective on events: disappointments in business are not worth dwelling on at the expense of family or health. Being with her family always helps her get through work disappointments.

Becoming comfortable in her own skin

If Terri were to meet her younger self today, she would feel quite disappointed that she was so held back by what other people thought of her. The conversation she'd have with her young self might go something like this:

'I wish you would be comfortable in your own skin, and just run your own race and stop trying to fit in with what everyone else is doing, because you are perfectly imperfect with your scratchy black skin and your skinny body or runny nose, whatever. All of that stuff is just an obstacle and you can run your own race around it. Run around it. Don't get bogged down in trying to seek other people's approval or to fit in. Don't worry about people trying to pigeonhole you; just be comfortable in your own skin.'

Naomi Simson

Rebel with a Cause

After a career in the corporate world with companies such as IBM and Apple, Naomi Simson established the online experiential gift retailer RedBalloon in 2001. The enterprise started as a one-woman business and is now Australia's leading online gift service, employing 60 people and offering over 3000 unique experiences across Australia and New Zealand. RedBalloon has been listed in the *BRW* fast lists six times, and was voted in the Top Ten Great Places to Work in Australia four years consecutively — one of only 13 organisations to have done so. Hewitt independently ranks RedBalloon with a 97 percent employee engagement score (the Australian average is 54 percent).

In 2011, Naomi was the Ernst & Young Entrepreneur of the Year in the Industry category and runner-up in the *BRW* Entrepreneur of the Year. In 2008, she was the national Telstra Business Women's Award winner for Innovation.

Naomi's blog is listed in the top 15 of Australia's Best Business Blogs. She is the author of *I Want What She's Having*, reviewed as an 'essential business read' by *The Australian*. Her most recent publication is *Five Thanks a Day*, a free book on the power of saying 'thank you'.

Major Turning Points

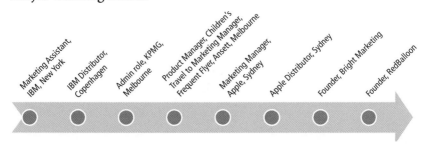

Marketing Assistant, IBM, New York

IBM Distributor, Copenhagen

Admin role, KPMG, Melbourne

Product Manager, Children's Travel to Marketing Manager, Frequent Flyer, Ansett, Melbourne

Marketing Manager, Apple, Sydney

Apple Distributor, Sydney

Founder, Bright Marketing

Founder, RedBalloon

Naomi Simson is widely known in Australia for two things: first, as the founder of RedBalloon; and, secondly, as someone who says what is on her mind, with a pull-no-punches approach.

A lot has been written about Naomi and RedBalloon; however, we've read and heard less about her earlier career, which is rich in examples of her fearless approach to business. This trait was certainly on full display when she was interviewed for this book.

While a single phrase could never do justice to Naomi's approach, the words *corporate nonconformist* spring to mind after listening to her recount her career trajectory.

Bewitched into marketing

'I'm not that clever — I was a Pass student.'

Naomi wanted to be an artist until her art teacher at school said, 'I can see you famous after you're dead, and starving in a garret.' The idea no longer appealed to Naomi, and she began exploring how she could use her creativity in a more commercial way. The solution emerged when she watched the 1970s television program *Bewitched*, in which one of the characters, Darren, was a commercial artist — leading her to consider advertising, then, with some coaxing from her mother, marketing.

In those days (the 1980s), Naomi could only obtain a marketing qualification through a commerce degree and could only complete a commerce degree by taking on accounting. So, as a budding artist, Naomi studied economics and commercial law with a sub-major in accounting, because she wanted to be creative. It sounds counterintuitive and probably would have horrified her art teacher, yet this non-creative track was where it started for Naomi.

Her father started his own business in the same year that Naomi, her sister and her mother all completed university qualifications! Naomi completed a Bachelor's degree in commerce; her sister, a qualification in speech pathology; and her mother, a postgraduate qualification in information management. Naomi recalls, 'Poor Papa, not only were we all at home, and he was working at home with three girls; it was absolute chaos and there was one phone line in those days.'

Discovering the world through IBM

In 1984, Naomi had the opportunity, as one of 72 graduates from around the world, to work for IBM in New York for 18 months through an exchange program via AIESEC, an international youth-run organisation offering young people the opportunity to participate in international exchanges and to live, work and study in foreign countries. She was in New York when IBM launched one of the first ever personal computers, the second-generation AT.

Moving to New York at 20 years of age was a big change and a great adventure. Having only ever travelled to New Zealand before, Naomi describes herself back then as a naïve puppy — so excited, happy and positive. Even when she was desperately homesick, she'd still say to herself, 'I wonder what today's going to bring?'

She assimilated quickly and within a week could no longer hear the American accent. Naomi was surprised at how unworldly Americans were at the time. One of her strangest experiences was offering a well-educated woman in the office a copy of an Australian newspaper (*The Age*). Realising that Australians spoke English, this woman then accused Naomi of lying to her about her ability to understand and speak English! 'She thought we spoke

Austrian or something … she thought I'd deceived her. And I was just like, "How?" I wasn't even playing tricks about kangaroos in the street or anything.'

IBM was very committed to the education and professional development of its employees, and Naomi felt she learned more in the 18 months she lived and worked in New York than she did at university. Her boss recognised her writing skills and gave her the opportunity to produce all the written reports for the division. This gave her exposure to very senior leaders within the organisation.

At the end of her 18-month term in New York, Naomi knew there were more exciting things to do than return to Australia. She had heard about trainees going to work for another computer company in California, known as Apple — 'I didn't even know there was another computer company!' However, Naomi had been offered a graduate posting in Copenhagen, Denmark, working for an IBM distributor, so she remained with IBM computers after travelling in South America for a little while. She returned to Australia with a 'nice-looking CV' and began looking for a job.

'Every time, I've resigned bosses'

Naomi got her first Australian job at one of the big four accounting firms in the country, cleaning their databases 'record by record'. She knew she did not have a career there. 'I couldn't write anything without my boss ripping it to shreds.' She left after one year; however, the best part of that time, recalls Naomi, is all the firm friends she made, many of whom she still keeps in touch with today.

To find her next role, Naomi selected five companies she would like to work for and sent them each her resume with a basket of fruit and a message that said something like, 'For this and more fresh ideas.'

She was offered jobs with three: Heinz Baked Beans, which was too far out in Doncaster from where she lived; ICI (now known as Orica), which was in the city and offered a generous salary; and Ansett, which paid the least but offered something she thought she could be passionate about — aviation. She took the Ansett job, although today she disparagingly describes the company at that time as a male-dominated, patriarchal, misogynist organisation ... so male that everyone thought she must have been a flight attendant because she was female.

> 'In those days people used to smoke in the office, and we had secretaries and we had a typing pool. And I would be in a meeting room, or somebody's office with one guy sitting — Mr Big Pin — on one side of the desk, and then all minions around. And they would all just smoke with the door closed. And I would sit and nearly die (as a non-smoker) and I couldn't say anything.'

She began at Ansett as the Product Manager for children's travel, before being promoted to Market Manager of the Golden Wing club program and then to Marketing Manager for Frequent Flyers. She often worked 15-hour days, yet she was still being paid about the same as when she started. One day, she plucked up the courage to ask a manager for a pay review, with her direct boss present at the meeting. 'He ripped strips off me. He said, "Who the hell do you think you are, coming into my office and demanding that we review your salary? I don't know what you do, and I don't give a damn. You just go and work until we tell you that we're ready to review your salary."' She left the office, went for a walk and burst into tears. But two weeks later, her direct boss successfully negotiated a pay rise for her: of five dollars a week. Naomi was so insulted by the meagre amount that she resigned — but not before she landed her next role at Apple.

'I decided there's somebody out there who wants my talents and my love.'

A sliding-door moment

Naomi moved to Sydney with Apple in 1992, as Marketing Manager in small/medium business marketing. She worked with the original founders of Apple in Australia at a time when an early project for them was to customise and distribute MYOB, an accounting software package. The company was tiny — perhaps only three people at the time. Naomi ran small business seminars around Australia to sell Macs with CD drives. At this point it was a situation of being in the right place at the right time; the Marketing Director left to start Vodafone in Australia, Naomi's boss was offered the Marketing Director's role, then she was given her boss's role as Marketing Manager for the publishing industry. At the time, this was Apple's core and most profitable business. Naomi describes the focus of the role as an almost evangelist one, talking about Apple's production-level computers for designers and publishers. As a result, she became a very sought-after resource at conferences and events. Eventually, she was approached to work for one of the distributors, and she was happy to leave because her fantastic manager had just been replaced by a 'dill'. It was time to resign the boss again, not the job, as Naomi puts it.

Naomi's corporate career in Australia began to develop one common theme: she left each of her jobs because of the bosses she worked for, not because of the job itself.

'Work–life balance is an oxymoron'

When she joined Apple, Naomi was newly married and had just moved to Sydney. Then, her husband, Peter, was told his business was being closed down. So Naomi became the sole income earner in a new marriage in a new city in a recession for a two-year period. What would have been a good salary in Melbourne was not in Sydney, with its expensive mortgages. She describes this time as full of an unbelievable sense of responsibility. Ultimately, Peter started his own accounting business, which he ran for two years, then sold it to Australian Business Limited, who agreed to keep him on for the next three years. With this development, suddenly they had a bit of financial freedom. It was at this stage that Naomi decided that, if Peter had three years of financial stability, she might step out and start a freelance marketing business.

Naomi's experience working briefly in a small distributor like Apple taught her that small businesses needed great marketing, but they could not afford it. Bright Marketing was pitched at this market.

As a new mum, Naomi had one precious hour with her daughter, Natalia, each day between getting home from work at five o'clock and her daughter's bedtime at six. She would have to leave work at 4.30 each day to ensure she would arrive by this time, which meant she never took breaks and was working every minute she wasn't with her children. The client base and income went from feast to famine and back again while Naomi just worked and worked throughout. After the birth of her second child, Oscar, she was with her kids every minute she could be, and then worked every minute that she wasn't.

'We only have one life; it's how we choose to spend it.'

Naomi quickly realised that she couldn't do it on her own. She employed a nanny who came nine to five every day because, as she put it:

> *'You can't be a mother and run a business … you're not doing justice to either. You're definitely not doing justice to your children. If they see you distracted and on the phone the whole the time, it's not fair to them, and they see it from the earliest age. And they understand where they sit in the pecking order.'*

Having a nanny at home and working from home meant she could choose to spend her time with the children. Thus, when she was with them, she was always fully present with them — she would have lunch with them, have bath time, play games, read, and generally be around. 'I did all the best bits and the nanny did all the hard stuff. But don't try and do both; it's just ridiculous.'

Bringing corporate lessons into her own business

> *'I'm grateful to all of them, and I've thanked them, in the chapter of my book "Thanks to all the No people". Thank you to all the people who told me I couldn't, I can't, I won't, I shouldn't; because of them, I chose to do what I do.'*

After almost two decades in the corporate world, Naomi learned some important lessons. For a start, the world of work is not necessarily a fair place; poor leadership abounds and great work is not always acknowledged or even appreciated. She believes a leader's job is to challenge people to achieve a greatness they didn't know they had within them. One of her favourite books, *The Multipliers*,[1] is about harnessing the energy and talent of people, and helping them to be bigger than they know themselves to be.

Naomi believes many leaders diminish people and they don't even know that they do it.

As a marketer, Naomi understood customer experience and brand experience, and recognised that creating a brand relies on relationships. When establishing her freelance marketing business, Bright Marketing, in 1995 she focused on a network of other freelancers she knew or had worked with and who would recommend her and bring business to her.

Being her own boss, she could hardly continue her pattern of leaving a job because of the boss! Yet the same theme of not being listened to was being played out in her own business. For instance, clients would pay her substantial fees for fabulous marketing plans and then pick off the pieces they liked one by one as if it was a shopping list, which destroyed the overall integrity and effectiveness of the plans. 'I found it unbelievably frustrating. I'd fall more in love with their businesses than they were, but they didn't have that innate commitment to customer experience, of which promotion was just a part. It wasn't the outcome [they were seeking].'

In some ways, starting RedBalloon in tandem with Bright Marketing was driven by Naomi's need to prove that marketing does work if you apply it consistently over and over without giving up. She has taken these lessons to heart and established RedBalloon as a workplace where everyone can do their best work and feel really proud. Her biggest fear now is 'everybody — employees and externals — think we should be in utopia and we will not be prepared for challenges or failures. Well, let's all get over ourselves,' says Naomi, 'because without bad times, you don't know good times. Without challenges, you don't know success.'

Not all success

Naomi has had her share of things that went wrong, including her last piece of consulting work with Bright Marketing, a job she had been so proud of. She was briefed to rebrand and rename a merged entity between Goldfields Ltd and Delta Gold, two long-established Australian gold-mining companies. Naomi facilitated workshops with the staff and with their leaders, and came to really understand the essence of the brand. They created a fabulous name, Aurion Gold, and a beautiful logo with the Southern Cross. She was very proud of it and considered it some of the best work they ever did. However, despite having done all the company searches, they were unaware that there was an energy company in Adelaide with a very similar name. Although adopting the new name, the Chairman and Managing Director of her client lost his trust in her because she hadn't been aware this other company existed. 'The saddest part was that, only three months later, a Canadian company bought them, and then the name disappeared altogether.' It was terribly sad and Naomi, having already launched RedBalloon by this stage and working in it part-time, decided she would focus on this new entity and turned away from consulting work forever.

Sexism

'RedBalloon is a very special place to work, and we don't see people's colours, sexuality — we're completely blind to all of those things. We just see wonderful human beings who are here to do their best work. That's all we see.'

Naomi is occasionally surprised when she reads how other corporate firms operate. She gives, as an example, law firms and their obsession with recording time as the basis of their billing system, rather than the intellectual contribution being made to the client. Many businesses create tournaments between staff where people must compete for resources, and Naomi believes you can't be a real team when you're competing, whether it be for resources or for anything else.

In the last two or three years, Naomi has been a member of an entrepreneur's organisation. She loved the fact that there were as many women as men, and she never saw herself as a female, just one of the players. When she left and joined a larger organisation for supposedly bigger players, she encountered more sexism then ever before. 'The worst thing is, they don't even know that they're being sexist.' Sometimes she experienced sexism from their wives. For instance, she was in a group of nine men once, and one of them said, 'My wife won't let me go and have a drink with you after work,' or, 'I can't invite you to the rugby.' One of the group said, 'My wife won't let me come here if you're here.'

Lessons for her younger self

'I was always very urgent about everything. Even in the first three or four years at RedBalloon, I'd start planning Christmas in February because Christmas is the biggest and busiest sales period for RedBalloon. One thing I would tell my younger self is, "There's going to be another Christmas." Also, to believe in myself, do it properly the first time, and trust that it might take two years, or three years, to get it done.'

Some of the men Naomi has worked with still say, 'Look, you're a bit outspoken. We're a bit worried about the fact that you blog. What are you going to write in those?' Or, 'You shouldn't be so high-profile. Somebody's going to pull you down a peg.' As Naomi puts it, 'People are still trying to tell me how to act and be — so I would say to my younger self, "Don't try and please other people. Just be really true to yourself. Know what you stand for, know what you believe in and absolutely chase after it." And you don't have to be friends with everyone.'

Steve Valmoss, Managing Director of Apple during Naomi's time there, said to Naomi recently, 'Look, I kind of remember you from Apple.' She said, 'Well, you probably just remember I used to ruffle everybody up the wrong way.' And he said, 'Yes.'

'I love being older. When you are older, you give yourself permission to choose who you want to spend time with; there are people who take energy and people who give it, or people with whom it's a level playing field. But at some point you can lose the takers.'

The advantage of being a woman in business

Being a woman in business has many advantages, in Naomi's experience. People are curious about why a woman is running RedBalloon, for instance, and she probably receives more exposure as a female than if she were male. Naomi also believes that women do bring different strengths to a business, such as empathy and believing in the good of all stakeholders, not just the shareholders.

Naomi was recently part of a conversation between her children in which her son asked her daughter if she would rather be a girl or a boy. Her daughter replied, 'I'd much rather be a boy … they don't have to work hard. They've just got to find a nice wife and they'll be happy ever after … Let's face it, if they've got a bit of a sense of humour and they can get along with people, a bloke's going to be okay. He doesn't have to work hard.' Naomi, who says she loves being a woman, was flabbergasted.

Meant to be: partners in work, not life

'I think it is far more interesting working with your ex-husband than your husband,' says Naomi. It has been nearly two years since she and Peter divorced. And for the first six months, going through that was really quite tough. But now they both sit on the board of RedBalloon together. 'The great thing is, I still love Peter, he's a great guy, but we probably were never meant to marry. In the end, he was just on such a different path than I was. And so he had to go and do what he had to go and do. He's a really, really good man, and I'm very happy to have such a great ex-husband. We probably talk more now than we did when we were married.'

The fact that they are opposite in many ways has probably helped make the business so successful. Peter, as an accountant, is very finance-focused and practical, whereas Naomi's focus is on engagement with people and changing the world. Peter keeps her grounded, challenging her and demanding answers like, 'Yes, but what about …' In the early days, if sales results did not come in on target, he'd say, 'So when are the sales coming?' The real challenge in running the business together was that they never left work, and work was always the topic of conversation.

The future

Naomi remembers the days when she was running Bright Marketing and the internet was just emerging. She wrote marketing plans for her clients, thinking, 'I'm a bit old to learn all about this internet thing.' Who would have thought back then that she would successfully create RedBalloon, an internet-based business, knowing very little about the internet. However, technology has never frightened her, perhaps because she has been around it most of her life — Naomi's mother worked on the first computer in Australia as a systems analyst and systems integrator for Aspect Computing.

What Naomi does know about the future is: if you create a brand that people love, it doesn't matter how or where it's executed; people are a part of your journey, and they're a part of your business.

> 'It's our customers who make us great; it's our suppliers who make us great. It's those who help us, who believe in us, who guarantee us our future. And it's our job to be the custodian for the brand experience. We're just custodians.'

Janine Allis
You've Come a Long Way, Baby

Boost Juice started in 2000 from a kitchen table in the suburbs of Melbourne. It now sells over one million juices and smoothies every month and goes through more than 50 tons of mangoes each year.

Not bad for a woman from the eastern suburbs who left school at 16, worked her way around the world in a range of down-and-dirty as well as glamorous jobs, then landed back in Australia with her husband and a great idea for a new business.

Janine has four children ranging from 21 to four years old. She is also bursting with good health, maintaining a five-day-a-week yoga practice and somehow fitting in surfing and tennis.

Major Turning Points

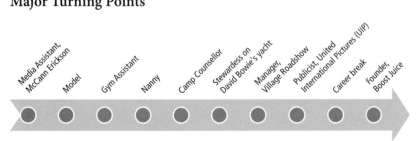

Media Assistant, McCann Erickson · Model · Gym Assistant · Nanny · Camp Counsellor · Stewardess on David Bowie's yacht · Manager, Village Roadshow · Publicist, United International Pictures (UIP) · Career break · Founder, Boost Juice

A confident and driven 16-year-old

It would not surprise anyone who has met Janine to learn that she was a very confident 16-year-old when she left school. At school, she did the bare minimum — didn't really put in any effort; never did any homework.

As the youngest of four children, she describes herself as just cruising under the radar when it came to homework. What was important to her was sport. University or any form of further education was never a consideration and not a conversation around the family table. All her friends left school after finishing tech school at 16 and went to work, so that was just the next logical step.

That is not to say Janine was not motivated or ambitious; she was very driven to pursue what she wanted and she wanted to get ahead. When she was 16 she wanted to work in advertising, so she would ring up advertising agencies and ask for jobs until she was offered a junior advertising role. When she was 21, all she wanted to do was travel, so she would work three or four jobs to earn enough money for her to go on an adventure overseas to see where life would take her. Then, when she returned to Australia, she wanted to get as far as she could possibly go in more corporate roles at Village Roadshow and UIP. That period included moving to Singapore with Village Roadshow to further her career and proactively find the right mentors or bosses to enable her to be the best she could be. However, the overriding consideration was to work in a job that she loved. She would never settle in a job where she was unhappy. Whenever she lost that interest, it was time to move on.

'It's a bit like boyfriends. I didn't actually hang on to them very long ... If I'm not enjoying it, I'll go and find something else.

And I had the confidence to just go and find something else,
and it'll be bigger and better.'

A spirit of adventure before entrepreneurism

Neither of Janine's parents was entrepreneurial or particularly
adventurous. She describes her family as a *Brady Bunch* sort of
family. Her father was a manager at Fibre Makers, earning just
enough to get by. His focus was the cricket and the football club.
Janine's mother was a stay-at-home mum. They lived very modestly
and very conservatively — owning a business was for someone else,
as that was considered far too risky for her family.

For a number of years, Janine took up opportunities as they
came — first, at Camp America in San Francisco for three
months, then from there went to Denmark with people she
had met. Travelling was fun and exciting, and taught her about
independence and resilience — the need to rely on herself to
find a solution no matter what. Travelling on her own meant
she was often put in precarious situations and had to rely on her
own resources to get out of situations, and work out how to get
from one country to the next by herself. She would draw on these
experiences and lessons when she came across problems in her
own business later in life.

After several years of travelling, Janine had had enough and
returned to Australia, settling in to a more traditional life and
corporate role with UIP. Her entrepreneurial spirit was fired up
when she met her partner, Jeff, who was entrepreneurial and
supportive, and then it flourished when she was on maternity leave.
Having a year off work enabled her to get off the treadmill of work,
reflect on what she really wanted to do, and evaluate other options
than going back to a corporate career.

Day one in the business: starting off with a bang

Twelve months prior to opening her first Boost Juice store, Jeff had been approached by an accountant and solicitor about a similar franchise concept in America and the rest is history. They sought Jeff out, Janine recalls, because he was a man, and they probably didn't trust her or thought she didn't have the nous to make it work because she was a woman. Nevertheless, Janine put the whole concept together, using her knowledge and IP to create Sejuice, the forerunner to Boost Juice, with these two business partners. This was a great lesson in the difficulties of a partnership. It did not work out as planned, so she and Jeff left the partnership to establish their own business (after a suitable long non-compete clause expired). Jeff found a great site in Adelaide even though they were based in Melbourne, and so the first Boost Juice store opened in Adelaide in 2000. They had a small marketing campaign, nothing extensive, and on the first day there was a massive queue and the store soon filled with people. Janine thought, 'How cool's this; this business isn't that hard.' She asked one of the ladies what led her to this store and was told there was a bomb scare next door, so everyone in that building was looking for a place to sit it out until they were allowed back in the building. Everyone had decided to try the new place that had just opened! Was that a serendipitous moment?

Their success can in part be attributed to the lucky (or wise) appointment of a fantastic first employee to manage the store. This enabled Janine to work on the business — establishing all the required systems, policies and processes early on, rather than having to work in the store. This experience contrasted with their first Melbourne-based store, which opened around 12 months later, on Chapel Street, South Yarra. This store had its own challenges because of its physical proximity to Jeff and Janine. Janine just couldn't help 'popping in' after hours as she walked past and working in the business, only to emerge hours later. So starting her first store interstate may have seemed strange and counterintuitive to some, but it had at least two key advantages: it was sufficiently geographically remote for Janine to allow the manager to manage and not to interfere with daily operations, plus it meant they were never daunted about opening other stores Australia-wide because they had already started interstate.

Early days at Boost Juice: one solution at a time

'There were days where every phone call was a negative and a disaster, and the next days, you know, the moon was in the right orbit and everything was good.'

After a great start to the business, not everything was smooth sailing. There were many times when Janine had to dig deep and apply the resourcefulness and problem-solving skills she had learned and applied while travelling overseas, to find a solution. There was many times when she thought she was lost or doubted herself, particularly in the first year when she didn't understand the business or the annual cycles the business goes through. But failure was never an option. She really needed that first year behind her to understand the dynamics of the business.

The rapid expansion of the brand in such a small business was a real challenge. The first few years involved constantly working out systems to make sure that things didn't fall through the cracks, which they inevitably did with such fast growth. One day after another involved working hard, opening stores, staffing them, getting them going, and making sure the supplier was there —

'all the billions of moving parts that it takes to actually make a business go' — and of course working out how to fix things that would go wrong.

'The tough times we had to have'

Janine admits that the huge success of the business as it went from zero to 120 stores in the first four years led to a level of arrogance. The blue skies, fantastic growth, great sales and the money pouring in the door led to a false sense of her own ability and her own importance. Yet you can't grow a business so rapidly and not have cracks. Two of the toughest periods for Boost Juice came about because of its own success. First, in April 2005, they encountered a period of bad public relations from a *Today Tonight* episode, which claimed that juices from Boost Juice contained more kilojoules than a can of Coca-Cola and one of Boost Juice's drinks had more calories than a Big Mac. Janine was naturally frustrated by this misleading news item, demonstrating that all her health juices and smoothies were healthier than soft drinks and that the comparisons were ludicrous. She believes this poor publicity was part of the sensational headline-grabbing nature of such TV shows, and targeting Boost Juice was based on the tall poppy syndrome. Nevertheless, the media latched on to the message, perceptions were affected, and sales were declining. Eventually, they worked with the TV station to come to an outcome that worked for both parties.

Secondly, because the brand was so hot, franchisees were coming in, selling them for an absolute premium. The banks were providing huge loans on the business that the cost of servicing the loans ripped out the profitability of the individual stores. So there were a lot of franchisees with profitable stores that were not being viable.

In hindsight, if it wasn't for the need to face up to the loss of revenue resulting from those situations, Boost Juice would not have the systems, processes and people to become the business it is today.

The negatives and setbacks were the times of greatest learning, much more than the periods of success. Janine strongly believes you learn more of what not to do from what has gone wrong, than you do from what has gone right. So really you have to have the setbacks.

'If you don't have setbacks, then you're not trying hard enough.'

Leapfrogging to future growth

With the business stabilised and 'all their ducks in a row', Janine and Jeff looked at the business's strengths and realised they are good at marketing — specifically, developing and growing a strong brand. They also had a business where all the foundations were as strong as they possibly could be, due in large part to Janine being a self-confessed 'control freak'. The next phase in their business would be to leverage these strengths. They have always loved the Mexican category, which they believe is a gap waiting to be exploited in Australia. They spotted Salsa, a fresh Mexican fast-food franchise. This category is a logical extension of their business, as it is all about delicious, healthy and fresh food, which is synergistic with Boost. They started with four stores and within three years grew that business to 37 stores. They have plans to open another twenty in 2013. This growth and expansion meant the business was becoming larger than the Boost Juice brand, so they created an umbrella business name, Retail Zoo. Armed with the learnings from Salsa and using the same business principles, in December 2012 Retail Zoo acquired Ciba Espresso, a chain of 20 stores in Adelaide.

Partners in love and work

Jeff was part-time in the business, working mainly on leasing and marketing. He was also working full-time in radio at the time — Janine describes Jeff as 'a real game-changer' in radio, and with his talent was able to position the Boost Juice brand very cleverly. About six years ago, he started to become more involved in the business. 'What's great about him is … we know each other's strengths and weaknesses, and we are very juxtaposed, which is fantastic. We are a good whole. The reason we work so well is we have the same work ethics. We work hard, we do what it takes, and we think on a similar path with regard to how business should work. I have my areas of expertise that I focus on, and really have the final say in those. And then he, in his areas, can make the final say. I think if one of us — it happens rarely — have a different view to the other one for various reasons, it's a heated debate, but we normally can work through it with logic. It's not about who's winning; it's about, "Why is this the right way to go, or why is that the right way to go?" And often when we're in those sorts of discussions, both ways are normally the right way; it's just one's a better way … you don't actually know which way is a better way until you actually go down a path.'

With both parents running the business, and two older sons, it would be natural to consider a family succession. However, Janine does not see the Retail Zoo being handed down to their children. She would rather see that they have taken the fruits from this business and given their children the opportunity to go on their own journeys, rather than always being in the shadow of their parents.

Janine is reluctant to give her children advice on their careers. She doesn't like being put on a pedestal by them and remembers a time when 'there was a big presentation and they were talking about business heroes. I was up there as a business hero, and Oliver, my 15-year-old, said, "I'm never going to be as good as that." And I went, "Aagh." I pointed out that he had better marks then me at school, he was smarter than me, he had his own path and dreams to pursue, and he should not put a barrier on them. He should not be comparing himself with me and his success may look different to mine.' Janine's message to him was: 'As soon as you go, "I can't," you won't.' She did not want him to ever think he couldn't be successful because he couldn't emulate her success.

Janine would rather her children did something that made them excited and opened their eyes, because that's a necessary ingredient for success — whatever success looks like.

Definition of success

As a 'successful female', Janine believes the debate about the low numbers of women in CEO roles and on boards is an interesting one. There are so many incredibly intelligent women that could easily be on boards or be CEOs of businesses, but may not be prepared to work the demanding hours it takes to be considered successful in these roles because some of that time is for spending with their children. Janine believes that often these huge board or CEO roles don't recognise that many women have parental drives as part of who they are. So a huge proportion of women are taken off that list of potential CEOs, or potential people on boards, despite having a hell of a lot to offer for some of those roles. But maybe because they've had that broken career they may not look as 'shiny' as people who have stayed in the workforce.

Being a woman is a bonus

However, in Janine's experience, being a woman has been more of a bonus than a negative. She cites, as an example, her membership to a very male-dominated Young President's Organization (YPO), with 50 men and only two women. The reason being female can be positive is that whether you are a client or a negotiator, 'They don't quite know what to do. You know, they're not sure where to put you. You're not the secretary, you're not the wife, you're not the mother, you're not the sister. So they don't quite know, because they're not used to dealing with women at a certain level. So you can play on that — you get the 50-year-old or 60-year-old guys who think that you're just this little girl and you need guidance, and I go, "Guide me all the way to where I want." So you use that: "I'm happy to be the girl that needs help, thank you very much." But I'm also very happy to be the woman that's very competent, and can do that too. So I need to get to X, and however I get to X, I don't really care, as long as I get there. And if I can't change you in a meeting, Mr Leasing 65-year-old Guy who thinks women should be in the kitchen, I can't change you, so I just work with that.' Janine sees the emotional intelligence and the flexibility of female thinking is the advantage women have over men — and, in her case, 'I had a business to run, I had a business to create and it was whatever it took to get that achieved.'

Breaking the glass ceiling

From Janine's perspective, having never worked in corporate institutions such as law firms or in finance, there does appear to be a barrier, or a glass ceiling, over women.

'But it seems like women seem to be able to break it, too. So I think, if you're as good as you can be, I don't think there is a

glass ceiling. You know what, there's always another business that there won't be a glass ceiling there for you, so if you are limited, then move.'

Janine's advice to anyone experiencing a 'glass ceiling' would be to move to somewhere that doesn't have one, just as several other women profiled in this book have done themselves.

'Maybe that's the only way for them to do it, because sometimes, as I said, there's a 55-year-old guy who ... might look at the woman and say, "You're at breeding age, you're going to leave us in a year," ... so it's difficult.

People often say to me, "You're so inspirational, you've done this and that," and I'm flattered, but the reality is that I am faulty. I don't always make the right decisions and I'm not always the person I want to be. I'm from Knoxfield and from a tech school. And, you know, I've worked my way up; I've had my little journey. Because of the media and because of the business, my name might be a little bit more known than, say, another person's name, but everyone has a story. Everyone has a great story.'

Lessons for her younger self

'I think one of the key things is that I was very influenced by people pretty quickly.' Janine offers the example of when she was travelling — 'I basically funded this one girl through her travels ... so I think I was quite gullible. But then again, do you grow up being cynical about everyone and their motives? That's sort of not a way to live, either. I think I'd just tell my younger self that it's okay to make mistakes; without mistakes, you can't grow.'

She adds: 'Don't get into strangers' cars!'

'I think, quite often, when you're a young person, luck plays an important part. I think you've got to go through all the stuff you need to go through. And when you think about it, I mean, everyone could think back on a long list of things that were just dumb, or stupid, or not something they'd be proud of. But without that you're not who you are today, and I like who I am today. So, in actual fact, I'd tell that girl to get on with it.

Yes, go for it. Just follow your path. Because luckily, you know, whoever was looking after that girl got her through all those areas that potentially other people may not have survived. And all of us have got stories where we could have gone that way instead of this way. Anything you take away on a journey affects where you are today.

I think I will always do something … I can't knit, so I can't imagine myself being an old lady not doing anything … I can imagine myself being an old lady being able to do amazing poses in yoga and having a healthy body and healthy mind and really contributing.

I think that life has a use-by date and I think you should live it.'

Farah Farouque

All Paths Lead Back to Social Justice

Farah is Senior Advisor, Public Affairs and Policy, for the Brotherhood of St Laurence, a newly created executive role in one of Australia's leading social welfare organisations. She came to this position with 20 years' experience as a journalist with *The Age*, covering national and Victorian politics, and social affairs, law and justice issues, as well as 'on the ground' reporting of critical international events such as the 2002 Bali bombings and the 2004 Boxing Day tsunami in Sri Lanka.

Her concern with social issues has led her to a number of pro bono roles in recent years, including as a founding board member of The Social Studio and as an advisory board member of The Global Health Gateway.

Farah was conferred a media award for excellence by the Victorian Multicultural Commission in 2008, and was a finalist for the Walkley Awards for Journalism in 2005.

Major Turning Points

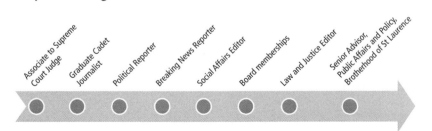

'There are things you do, as a citizen'

Farah was always aware of these 'things', even as a small child.
The eldest of seven children born to Sri Lankan parents, an early
memory centres on the efforts of her mother and a group of other
women to enable a young local woman to get married. It was a
small gesture, but resonated in Farah's mind. Wedding finery is
a cultural requirement in the South Asian context but is often
beyond the financial means for many poor families. This girl came
from such a family and had nothing to wear for her own wedding.
The women sourced clothes and other finery, including loaning
some of Farah's mother's own jewellery, for the wedding.

Farah's father was a senior public servant in the Sri Lankan
government and had been a Fulbright Scholar at Columbia
University in the US. Her mother was a university graduate, and
had taught in the United Nations preschool in New York and done
social welfare work in Sri Lanka. 'My family was well-off, relative
to the rest of society. I grew up in an unequal, hierarchical society.'
But within the household there was no inequality. Her parents
were as equally ambitious for their daughters as for their sons, and
encouraged all their children to succeed. Her grandmother was
also an intelligent woman. Although tied down by the traditions
of her generation and culture, her ambitions were transferred onto
her oldest granddaughter. When Farah announced one day that she
wanted to be an air hostess, her grandmother, who had not been
allowed to finish high school, told her off and said she should be
a doctor.

When the family migrated to Adelaide in the mid-1970s,
Farah's father was an academic at the University of Adelaide. Her
mother focused on bringing up children, but did voluntary and
community work.

*'I grew up in a home where a job wasn't just about earning
money and thinking about yourself ... There are other things
you do, as a citizen. I think that background informed my
sense of contributing to a broader purpose ...'*

'I was comfortable in that public space'

When it came to Farah's time to consider tertiary education and
careers, it was the humanities that she was interested in. Her father
encouraged her to study law so she did a double degree in law and
arts, majoring in politics and history.

Once enrolled at the University of Adelaide, she threw
herself into the extracurricular activities, probably more so than
the curriculum itself. 'I joined the Legal Aid Society and I did
voluntary legal aid work. I was always a school debater, and in my
first year I was secretary of the campus debating society, and then I
became president the next year. I was quite an active contributor in
that sense.' Her first job after graduating was as a judge's associate in
the Supreme Court of South Australia. She provided legal research
and professional support to the late Justice Mohr, whom she had
met through a part-time job. She obviously impressed him enough
on the occasion for him to promptly invite her onto his staff. 'It was
a good opportunity, and that probably finessed my resume.'

However, Farah had largely decided that she was not going
to make law her career, as 'law and the mechanics of it would
probably not be a perfect fit for my personality, which tends
towards the kinetic'. A close friend had suggested journalism to
her, and Farah felt it was in that sphere that she could become fully
engaged in the political and social issues that concerned her.

'You can't just decide you want to be a journalist; you've got to
start doing some journalistic work,' and Farah had already made

a start. She had grasped at the opportunities that were available during her student years, including voluntary work as a newsreader at an ethnic community radio station and becoming a contributor to the university newspaper.

Farah had always had things to say for herself, even as an 11-year-old. When she was in primary school, Channel Seven television selected a number of children from several demographically different primary schools in Adelaide. Ten of them, including Farah, went on to present a current affairs and sketch revue program that lasted for a couple of years.

Although, at the time, she did not think of being a journalist, the TV experience fitted well with her developing interests. 'I was comfortable in that public space, I suppose.'

Succeeding in a white, Anglo-Saxon man's world

As a well-educated woman who was fortunate to be provided with a good start in life, Farah never felt she was treated differently because of her ethnicity (Sri Lankan) or her religious background (Muslim). To the contrary, she believes her cultural difference provides her with a greater awareness and understanding of other perspectives. She was often seen as a mediator on these issues in the newsroom, too, being the 'go-to' person on issues of diversity and cultural difference. She strongly believes that having a diverse background, whether of colour or religion or culture, can help make you 'more alive to nuances' but should not limit you.

If anything, being a woman was more of a stumbling block for Farah during her career in journalism. Newsrooms remain a very male-ordered culture, which can be hostile to women. The numerical dominance of men in key decision-making roles in the media creating a 'bloke' or masculine culture has been researched and documented elsewhere,[1] and it remains a battleground for women who need to fight for coverage of 'women's issues' such as childcare. Farah acknowledged that the general atmosphere of a newsroom is that 'men prosper more than women in the higher echelons of management', but this has not been her experience in the practical application of journalism, where good reporting speaks for itself. Farah's media awards are testament to this: they include Victoria's Multicultural Awards for Excellence (Media) in 2008, and being a finalist for the Walkley Awards for Journalism in 2005.

Farah believes women need to carefully plot their life course in the context of their career. 'I'm a single woman; if I had children I may have had a different career pathway. For instance, if I had childcare responsibilities, I might not have been able to so easily go and cover a tsunami with a few hours' notice.' Some of her peers who have children have had to make different choices. Farah does not say this with any regret — just a pragmatism that comes with the need to balance priorities in one's life.

Motivations, preparations and learning from work

Farah's motivations come from her desire to be successful, rather than from any singular ambition. There was never a corporate position or management track to be attained, for her career choices were more a considered question of deciding what her interests were and then setting out to be successful in that role — 'I wanted to do what I wanted to do.'

This type of motivation requires planning as much as any other type, and Farah was a master of planning from the very beginning. Having decided she wanted to go to Melbourne and work at *The Age* newspaper, which in the early 1990s required sitting a written general knowledge exam before several interviews, Farah travelled to Melbourne on a reconnaissance mission several months before the exam time. She spent the week travelling on trams and acclimatising herself to Melbourne life. 'I remember even taking myself to lunch at Mietta's.' When she returned home to Adelaide, she started an intense period of reading on Victorian history and politics. She passed the exam and began her graduate cadetship.

All the planning in the world cannot prepare you for everything, however, and 'joining the workplace was a bit of a rude shock'. Automatic annual pay rises, for example, were not as automatic as Farah had thought, and she had to learn to lobby for one herself.

'I was smart about how to get in, but it took me some years to learn to navigate the rules of the workplace.'

Farah's desire to work in her area of interest and to be successful continued to be her driving force. Within a couple of years she was posted to the Canberra bureau. She was a junior, 'the lowest of the 10 people out there, so it wasn't exactly a prestigious posting, but it was a great opportunity'. This posting gave her the chance to rub shoulders with the likes of Michelle Grattan (then Political Editor of *The Age*) and Mark Baker (National Editor). Before getting the Canberra job, Farah laughingly remembers orchestrating 'a really pathetic little ruse' to enhance her prospects of being picked for a posting. She saw Michelle Grattan leaving the building in Melbourne so decided to time her own departure and join the editor in the lift. 'I don't think I made any impact on her whatsoever ... I probably erred on the side of being overenthusiastic [with these types of approaches], but it didn't hurt me in the long run.' Mark Baker became a good mentor to her in Canberra, in what was otherwise a formidable atmosphere to be working in as a junior journalist. One problem was the heady exposure to large political figures. Farah reflects that it is probably not a good idea for journalists to be excited about their job as 'you shouldn't be impressed by the people you cover'.

As exciting as Canberra was, in some respects it was a place where journalists had to 'live and breathe work', and Farah realised that she was not prepared to live that way. 'Friends and family have always been very important to me. I've never dropped the ball in that area … I'm not one of those people who spend every moment of the day thinking about work. Downtime is vital to remain grounded.' So she moved back to Melbourne and covered state politics for a year or so. However, after the intensity of Canberra, she was not as engaged in the state issues as she could have been.

This period led her to what was probably the first real learning Farah took from her work.

> 'I came to the conclusion that sometimes you don't have to
> have a goal. You can do your current task well, and that can
> be … quite satisfying, if you do a good job, and you write
> well or whatever it is you do … I became more mature in
> my attitude to work.'

She moved into the general pool of reporters after this, at her boss's request, and after a few months came to really enjoy this work despite having resisted the move at first. It was a very broad role with every day being as unpredictable as the one before. 'The moral I take from that particular phase of my career is that sometimes you may not make particular choices, but you must make the best of them and they can turn out to be the best move you ever made.'

This was the case for Farah, who treated these five years of general reporting as a springboard for other opportunities, including a three-month Asialink–University of Melbourne fellowship posting to Jakarta. An appointment as *The Age*'s Social Affairs Editor, leading a team of reporters, was her next and her longest role in journalism. Social policy issues including poverty, child protection, demographic changes, cultural diversity and gender issues were all within her gamut. 'They weren't trendy issues,' but Farah considered it a challenge to do well with them and is satisfied that she did. It was in this phase that Farah also acquired new skills as a senior editor, regularly filling in and managing staff for the Saturday current affairs feature section 'Insight', and as Acting Opinion Editor for the daily paper. Although she resisted the management pathway preferring to be a writer, she was also regularly called on to act in chief-of-staff roles for the entire newsroom.

It was during these years that Farah also had two of her most challenging assignments as a journalist. The first was in 2004, when she was sent to Sri Lanka to cover the effects of the Boxing Day tsunami, and the second was four years later when a 15-year-old boy was shot by police during a confrontation at a skate park in Melbourne's inner north. Both were shocking incidents at different levels and for different reasons that were very human and community-based. Her reporting of the Boxing Day tsunami was for the *Sydney Morning Herald* as well as *The Age*, and received a nomination for the prestigious Walkley Awards.

Support is more important than formal mentors

Some of Farah's work challenges arose in her role as a team leader rather than as reporter and writer. She had learned over the years that to be a nurturing type of leader was important, as is supporting others by being a sounding board for ideas or concerns. 'My advice may not have been useful. I must confess I liked to offer advice based on my own experiences, but people ultimately make their own decisions, and they are independent actors in these matters … I tried to be a sounding board especially for other women, and to encourage them to achieve.'

Farah does not attribute her achievements as a journalist to the type of mentoring support that is becoming quite common in corporations these days, whereby a more junior, aspiring individual is mentored by a more senior leader in the business. The need for a formal, upwards relationship is not always required. A more equal relationship worked more effectively for Farah, and she sought and received greater support from her peers and friends than 'up the food chain'. A high self-belief and high levels of self-motivation also kept Farah grounded and focused.

Becoming involved in the issues

Towards the last few years of Farah's career in journalism, she began to develop the confidence and desire to become more involved in other things outside her work. This reflected her parent's attitude to life and the way Farah had been brought up, although, she remarks, 'to be honest, as a journalist you probably shouldn't be too identified with single issues'. However, when she was approached to join the board of an emerging social enterprise in Melbourne, it became an opportunity to contribute to issues relating to diversity, ethnicity and multiculturalism that had always been important to her. The Social Studio, a social enterprise in Melbourne's inner north, was founded to break down the barriers of unemployment, isolation, education and training for young refugees by instigating supportive projects grounded in formal training in clothing production, retail and hospitality.[2]

> 'I derived a whole new dimension from my community activities. I enjoyed journalism, but this felt really good ...'

Farah has also joined the advisory board of Global Health Gateway, an online forum for connecting people who have an interest in global health issues with opportunities for training, employment and volunteering.

As these opportunities became more fulfilling, and as the world of journalism as Farah had known it was rapidly changing with several rounds of staff redundancies and the migration to online media, it became timely to consider a change in career. While it was always something in the back of her mind, after 20 years as a journalist this was not an easy decision to make and she consulted trusted friends and professional contacts before making her choice. The voluntary redundancy package offered was financially attractive, which made it easier to take the leap.

Farah's intention was to take up to a year to plot a new career in the social policy arena. However, the newly created position of Senior Advisor, Public Affairs and Policy, with the not-for-profit Brotherhood of St Laurence was advertised and Farah applied for it. A month after taking redundancy, she was offered the position. The issues around tackling poverty were important to her, and the public advocacy part of the job required some media experience, but the new brief was much broader than journalism: it fit all Farah's requirements for a new challenge.

**Finding the similarities rather than the differences
when transitioning across sectors**

A significant career change involving a new sector and new role
after 20 years of success in journalism is somewhat of a gamble
for anyone, despite it being the right time to move from a rational
perspective. Not many individuals have crossed over from the
newsroom to the community sector. The leap into a new sector
required Farah to be able to back herself, to examine her personal
strengths, weaknesses, opportunities and limitations, and to seize
opportunities that matched her package of capabilities, rather than
being held back by perceived obstacles. She describes her role as
a fusion of her media experience (public affairs part of the role)
where the transition to the community sector is a fairly natural
one, combined with a new area of public policy.

Three months into the new role, Farah is positive about the
transition. She enjoys the new challenge and the opportunity
to be engaged with issues on a deeper structural level. She does
not miss the seemingly 'glamorous' and high-profile world of
journalism, including the constant drama and energy that abounds
with journalists and the media scrum. She seems to have fitted
comfortably into the community sector and sees many similarities
across these sectors. For one thing, the community sector is not the
dour sector some people may perceive it to be. People there are very
determined and purposeful but also passionate and committed, just
like many journalists she has worked with. Also both sectors are
content-driven, although the community sector tends to be more so,
and engaged on a more serious structural level.

Working in the community sector has nevertheless exposed
Farah to some differences in culture and approach and has
demanded some adjustments in approach as well as the application

of some new skills. One challenge has been shifting to a more long-term focus. In her last role, as Law and Justice Editor, for example, Farah focused more on the 'short game'. Here, she would focus on one or two stories at a time and move from one event to the next after a clearly defined period of time. Contrast this with the community sector 'long game', where she needs to be across a whole range of serious issues that intersect and play out over a much longer timeframe. This requires a more measured approach, rather than judging an issue by whether something is a good story that can run in tomorrow's paper.

Another difference is the need for Farah to adapt to a more structured approach to her work —in journalism, Farah may run with a story intuitively, quickly and pretty much on her own. In the Brotherhood of St Laurence, the focus is more considered, requires more consultation, and involves the preparation of structured presentations and papers for meetings. Work is done in a more collegiate way, too.

'What I know now': lessons for her younger self

If Farah could talk to her younger self she might say, 'Go after your goals and always maintain the balance; don't make work all-consuming. It is really important to have family and friends.'

Farah believes that gender difficulties have eased somewhat but 'there are certain assumptions in the workplace' that mean women have to work harder than men to get ahead. The institutional or systemic barriers are no longer there, but even with the same abilities, skills and aspirations it is still a lot easier for males than it is for females, and this disparity is reflected in the pay packet.

However, putting gender issues aside, the current world of work tends to be a difficult place for many people, particularly if they are not resilient. The advice she gives people is that most contexts at work do not resemble the comfortable womb of university, which she felt to be more nurturing. 'You feel that you can do anything, but actually, in the world of work, there are many more barriers. It's not all about ability or merit, that's the big thing. Cream doesn't always rise to the top. Office politics can get in the way of good intentions or merit-based promotions.' She adds:

> 'To be a successful person at work, it isn't just about being very good at your job, or competent. It's about personal skills, networking, getting on with people, impressing the right people and finding the right mentors.'

Farah believes that, early on in her journalistic career, she could have perhaps invested more time and effort networking and managing up within the workplace. 'When I started I had a certain naïveté about me that did not serve me well; it obviously helps to wise up early to the ways of work but, with time, everyone gets better at the often subtle internal politics of securing advancement. You can learn to be strategic.'

More generally, though, Farah is of the belief that the main prerequisite to a person's success is access to a good education. However, while skills and competence, along with working hard, are important, you also have to be flexible and adaptable in your thinking at work. 'If work and life throws you a curve ball, don't always resist it — it can take you to many challenging places.'

Jane Fenton, AM
Planned Happenstance

Jane Fenton, AM, is the founder of Fenton Communications, a Melbourne-based public relations and marketing communications consultancy. A Victorian Telstra Business Women's Award winner, she is also a Member of the Order of Australia (AM) for services to the community, particularly through support for a range of health, medical research, youth and women's groups.

Jane has been a pioneer on many occasions. She was the first Public Relations Officer at the Law Institute of Victoria. She was a pioneer in the public relations arena, convincing law firms of the importance of marketing and advertising themselves and their practices, and established the first professional services firms marketing firm.

She was one of the first to convince the community sector of the importance of public relations, marketing communications and stakeholder engagement, and has morphed her business to focus on the service sector and on issues that are important to the community: health, social justice, education and sustainability.

Jane is a member of the board of Cancer Council Australia, a former Chair of the Victorian Health Promotion Foundation (VicHealth), a past President and Life Governor of Very Special Kids, and a former board member of the Murdoch Children's Research Institute.

Major Turning Points

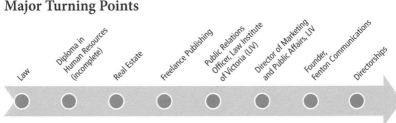

Law · Diploma in Human Resources (incomplete) · Real Estate · Freelance Publishing · Public Relations Officer, Law Institute of Victoria (LIV) · Director of Marketing and Public Affairs, LIV · Founder, Fenton Communications · Directorships

Traditional expectations

'Every step has been a tentative pulling away from that
predominant factor of traditional expectations.'

Family, being a decent human being, economic security and
being happy — these were what Jane's parents wanted for their
children. Her father had very traditional views about men and
women. As a farmer, he believed the farm would be passed on
to the men, and women should get married and have children.
A career was certainly not for women, while work itself was to
provide security for life and a pension for retirement. Above all,
he believed it did not matter what job his daughter ended up
with, even the 'dustbin person', as long as she was polite to people
and a decent human being.

Jane did not fulfil her father's understandings of a woman's role
in society, and described every step she made as a tentative step
away from what her father thought was important. Yet before he
died he apologised for his attitudes when his children were young
and said he was so proud of all that his daughters had achieved.
Her mother, a nurse prior to her marriage, was a very values-
driven person. She just wanted all her children to be happy, so it
was for them to determine where happiness lay.

Jane believes she was extremely lucky to have parents who
were very accepting and trusting. 'Nobody said, "You can't. We
won't let you."' When she said she was coming to Australia to live,
nobody said no. 'Nobody said, "You can't go." Nobody said, "Are
you sure?" My parents said, "Well, if that's what you want to do,
off you go."' Yet, looking back on it, Jane describes this decision as
rather cruel to her parents on her part — her mother was younger
than Jane is today.

Jane's upbringing is fairly typical for women of her generation, and many continue to experience strong gender-influenced attitudes throughout their working lives. However, she does not believe that was the case for her. She had been to an all-girls school; then to law school, where half the students were women; and at home, despite her father holding strong views about a woman's role in the family, she and her sisters were never treated differently than her brothers on a day-to-day basis. Throughout her business life she feels privileged that gender has never been a barrier, except for one relatively small situation earlier in her career. One of her colleagues did everything possible to put her down in front of others without actually crossing the line of saying things she could complain about, which was infuriating. But, in the end, Jane knew she was doing a good job and was not going to let it get her down or let it stand in the way of what she wanted to do.

Jane sees many women in large organisations experiencing blatant stereotyping and discrimination, and does not diminish the impact of these experiences on women. Other women's experiences remind Jane of how fortunate she was. However, to a large extent, she had created situations where she was in control of her own destiny, especially in establishing and successfully leading her own business, so she had not been exposed to these practices to the same extent as other women who perhaps had less choice. She also believes that, as a consultant, companies employ you for your skill set, and gender becomes less relevant. Being the only female in a room full of men, it often helps to be able to bring a different voice, a different presence and a different approach. And where she feels the values of the organisation don't fit with her own, she will not undertake work for them.

For Jane, the career path she took was guided by a practical realisation rather than rebellion against a perceived stereotype. She knew she wouldn't inherit the farm, and, despite her father's view that women should get married, at that stage she wasn't so sure marriage was going to be a pathway for her. 'I knew I'd have to fend for myself. So, I decided to use the best of my ability to … be independent.' Jane did marry, at nearly 40 years of age. She reflects that it would have been a 'fairly disastrous life' had she waited for marriage as her father wanted. In one of many examples of serendipity throughout Jane's life, she views her relatively late marriage as a bonus. At that stage in life, both partners are much clearer about what's important to them, and the patterns of their life and work are clear. Jane feels they 'probably avoided a lot of the tensions relationships have when they go through those business establishment phases'.

Jane also sees much of her career path as being guided by happenstance and choice-making, and the important thing for her is to make the most of one's experiences and lessons in a positive way.

She enrolled in law school believing her career was mapped out for her. She had a fairly idealistic view of law: she was 'going to wear the wig and gown and be a barrister and hopefully change the world in this forum'. But she soon realised that maybe she wasn't the right person for this work — her strong sense of the importance of justice, stemming from her parents' teachings to be a decent human being, happy and values-driven, struggled as she began to realise 'that law and justice are two completely different things'. Enforcing the law does not necessarily mean achieving justice in all cases, and she became disillusioned.

Feeling more and more like a 'square peg in a round hole' and with no professionals in the family to guide her, Jane decided to pursue her passion for justice by aligning her law studies with an interest in industrial relations and social justice, so she enrolled in a Postgraduate Diploma in Human Resources.

In the first major example of the importance of making choices, Jane received an opportunity to travel to Australia for a holiday and decided to defer the final assignment, which was to be completed as a work placement. She came here, fell in love with Australia and decided to live here rather than complete her qualification. Leaving England also meant giving up a hard-fought-for graduate trainee position with the National Health Service, something she was to start once her final assignment had been completed and she had her postgraduate diploma. She felt bad about declining this position, as she had fought very hard for it — there were only a small number of graduates selected in the whole of England. However, her rationale was, 'I decided that this was too good an opportunity to miss … things happen and opportunities present themselves and sometimes you have to be prepared to give up something that you had thought was really important in order to take advantage of the here and now.'

Having burnt her bridges with both the diploma and her postgraduate job, Jane returned to the UK for 12 months to do whatever work she could find and earn enough money to come back to Australia. These jobs included 'the worst job I ever had in my life', selling cheap short-term rentals in properties owned by landlords who were blatantly racist and only wanted to offer their apartments to white non-UK nationals. 'I was paid on commission so I lasted six weeks and learnt nothing, but it was a good eye-opener for me.' Jane did, in fact, learn what she didn't want to do: she would never be a good salesperson, she couldn't force people to do things they didn't want to, and the sheer prejudices of the landlords and desperation of some of the renters awoke in her a very clear sense of injustice. She then worked in a publisher's firm for a year and that provided her with the money to return to Australia.

'Everything I've done, I value enormously'

Once Jane returned to Australia, she commenced a freelance job in publishing, travelled around Australia, had a fabulous time, ran out of money, and then successfully applied for a job at the Law Institute of Victoria (LIV). This was a dream run for a 20-something law graduate wanting to make a new life in a new country.

The job was as Public Relations Officer, a role the LIV hadn't had before. This was extraordinary, says Jane, because 'they didn't know what a public relations officer did and neither did I, but typically for lawyers, they were more comfortable with someone who had a law degree than with someone who had a public relations qualification.'

Jane describes this role as 'the best job in the world' because, as it was a new role, she was allowed to make the job whatever she thought it needed to be. She had the opportunity to get heavily involved in advocacy, including working on a campaign to build the remand centre and alleviating the many problems associated with sending remand prisoners to Pentridge Prison.

Her law degree was what clinched this job and, although it did not lead to a traditional legal career, it was being utilised in a setting that enabled her to make the most of her writing and publication skills. It also taught her the discipline of thinking in a logical and factual manner and in a way that applied respective precedent. Her legal perspective has over the years made a huge difference to the way she frames things. Jane describes herself as a fairly emotional person and believes her law degree provided her with a disciplined way of thinking, and helped her conceive of an argument, understand the basis for assumptions and use research to get to a point. Communication can very easily be loose and glib, so Jane's disciplined thinking helped to sharpen up the messages.

After about three years, Jane was promoted to the position of Director of Marketing and Public Affairs, which she did for another couple of fruitful and rewarding years.

'I don't think that being comfortable is what life is about'

'Focus has held me in all my steps.'

Jane had had a fantastic five years in which she had the privilege of inventing her own role twice: as Public Relations Officer, and in marketing and public affairs. However, she was unable to progress further at the LIV, as she had neither the requisite experience nor the qualifications for the only more senior role: that of the CEO. She was young and felt it was time to move on. Yet she could not think of another company she wanted to work for.

The next step was really quite a logical one for her. One of the areas in the legal profession in which she'd begun to make a difference while at the LIV was in changes to the *Legal Profession Act*, removing the restrictions around marketing and enabling lawyers to act more like businesspeople by advertising themselves and their practices. Armed with these legislative changes, Jane was able to show lawyers that they could be both a professional, with all the hallmarks of a professional, and a businessperson. Reflecting on how the legal profession has subsequently changed since these restrictions were lifted, Jane doesn't necessarily like the direction marketing has taken some law firms, but she still believes that 'as long as they meet their professional obligations, they should be able to go out there and present themselves to the market'.

Here was something she could do: help lawyers communicate their businesses, their abilities and their specialties to the market. So Jane and Max, another director at the LIV, went into business together to do marketing, public relations and communications for lawyers. They were both so excited but made all the mistakes many people make when they go into business.

'It was the best and stupidest decision that I've ever made in my life,' says Jane. The decision was made with no business plan, no money, no clients, a single shared computer and a profession that didn't want to buy the service they had to offer. However, when Jane looks back, she considers it the best time of her life.

This was because she was forced to learn how to focus on one thing despite the pressures that life dealt her on all fronts. Regardless of the family, business, personal or 'giving to the community' pressures, 'you just knew the only thing that you had to do was find a way of getting work'. Jane had no immediate family here, so she had to make it work on her own. To top it off, knowing that no bank would lend money to a single woman who was not gainfully employed, the last thing she did before leaving her job was buy a cottage, with interest rates at 17.5 percent at the time. Financial pressures — you bet!

The work Jane and Max did when they started out was mostly about teaching lawyers client service — how to get repeat business, how to look after existing clients in order to get referrals or more work — as well as managing their profile by writing newsletters and brochures, and undertaking some PR for them. Back in 1972, when the business started, they were radically new concepts, which is difficult to imagine today when many of the top-tier firms have large teams of marketing people.

The pair worked together for three years before deciding, amicably, to split the business and go in different directions. They split because they never had the conversations they should have had at the beginning regarding business planning, their preferred styles and the level of risk each were prepared to take on. As a result, every now and then it became clear to them both that they were approaching their business with a totally different understanding. For instance, Jane required little more than enough money for her mortgage and wanted to build something slowly. She also describes herself as an extreme introvert. Max, on the other hand, had bigger and faster plans than that and was aiming for 'the big picture', something that scared her because 'I was worried about doing things I didn't think I knew how to do. He was a wonderful extrovert.'

Despite these differences in outlook, she believes they were a really good combination because she could take care of the follow-up and the detail, while Max was a big-picture thinker and could step back and make plans for them both. But without the important discussions, 'we both assumed a whole pile of things, and it wasn't until something went wrong that you would say, "Well, how could you possibly think that?" and we realised we hadn't had any of the right discussions.'

The fact that they were congenially able to divide up the client base demonstrated how different their approaches to clients really were. Each client preferred one style and mode of operating over the other, and so clearly preferred working with either Jane or Max. She is very proud to say that she and Max are still friends today.

One of the most difficult decisions of Jane's work life came at this time, when they had to let a couple of staff go. It was critical to the survival of the business to make staff redundant. For Jane, it is the most difficult, painful, unpleasant thing she has ever done, but she is conscious that for the sake of the other people in the business you have to make those tough decisions; that was the first learning for her.

It never occurred to Jane to that she might actually have to tell somebody they no longer had a job. It didn't get any easier, but it was a principle that she learnt very early — in small business, you always know the people really well so it is more difficult than in big business. 'You know their financial situation, you know their personal situation, you know their family's names, you've met their children, you know the name of their dog, but you still have to make the decision that's the right decision for the business.'

As with her law degree, Jane views this partnership as an experience about which she has absolutely no regrets. Jane believes there is something to be learnt from every experience, and one of the things she learnt from these years with Max was courage. 'I learnt so much from him about courage that, at the time, I didn't know how to exercise. I've still since, I think, learnt from that, embracing completely new things, giving it a go.'

Despite not considering herself to have the courage for the big business Max was aiming for, Jane nevertheless decided to continue consulting after they split up and went out on her own. Fenton Communications is still going strong 25 years later.

While Jane believes that being 'uncomfortable' helps with learning to focus on what really matters, it also helps to have support and she credits two people with providing 'critical' help. On her arrival in Australia, her aunt (her mother was originally Australian) took Jane under her wing and was a strong female presence in her life. When she and Max split the business and Jane continued as a sole consultant, the second important influence was a woman who was also establishing her own small business. She had the bright idea of establishing a network of women with similar aspirations. 'We didn't market to each other or sell services across the network, but we'd talk about who's got a good accountant, how you found the right staff or how to solve any of the myriad of problems we faced … We kept going for about four years and I regard that network as being critical … it was a safe space you could go to, women who get together with common interests and common views … we used to buy a cheap bottle of plonk because it was all we could afford and we would sit around the table and we helped each other. It was great.'

The switch: using business for community work

Fairly early on in the life of Fenton Communications, Jane began doing voluntary work with community organisations. Very Special Kids was her first experience. She then joined the Children's Hospital Research Foundation, later the Murdoch Children's Research Institute. 'One day I asked myself why I was spending all my spare time involved in organisations and sectors that I was really enjoying, while at the same time I was losing my sense of enjoyment out of my traditional consulting work.' Jane decided to flip her business on its head and direct it towards the community work she was more engaged in. 'Most people, I think, use their business as a springboard to what they do in the community, but it was actually my community involvement that made me say, "I can do something better in the business."'

Jane was enjoying marketing legal services less and less, and this loss of satisfaction in the business spurred Jane on to change the nature of her business. So she reframed the business and began broadening her work to include areas she was passionate about — including not-for-profit organisations alongside her health work, followed by education, then, as time went on, sustainability. She was working in all of what she regards as the major societal issues in the business. The business would not have developed that way, Jane believes, if she had followed a straight pathway of making business decisions based purely on business considerations.

The unorthodoxy of this approach was pointed out to Jane on a visit she made to her accountants several years ago. She went to talk about future directions and business and succession planning. Her accountant asked her to write the headlines that she would like to see about her business in 10 years' time, so she wrote several examples that highlighted Fenton's reputation, winning a prize for something, and contributions to the community. The accountant said, 'Where is the "goes public", "makes a million dollars' profit a year", et cetera, et cetera?' Jane saw this as a very helpful exercise. 'It was good for me as a reminder, and I do completely understand the importance of profit and business and all of that, but it was just what my focus was.'

And this focus was to reward her with something so much more than a million dollars in profit. In January 2004, Jane was awarded a Member of the Order of Australia 'for service to the community, particularly through support for a range of health, medical research, youth and women's groups'. For Jane, it was a 'hugely significant moment' and a 'beautiful recognition' because it showed that she could use her business and her skills to make a significant contribution to the community — in her words: 'that you could be in a small business and life didn't all have to be just about the business; you could really connect those two things'.

The ethos of Fenton Communications was always to make these types of significant contributions in the form of pro bono work and support. 'I did the figures and we've put millions "with an *s*" back over the years, in terms of free services and contributions and the like. So, for me, that's the pleasure of business. You have to have a successful business and you have to make it profitable, it has to work; but then what you choose to do with that, that's where the choice comes in, and that's where I've enjoyed exercising that choice.'

Being honest with herself

'When you start to think about something and put the vibe out there, without even saying anything, things start to happen.'

Part of the future directions Jane discussed with her accountant was also a consideration of what she herself might do over the rest of her working life. She had previously appointed 'the most fabulous person' to take the lead from her in the business when the time came, so Jane began to think about her own skill set, what she had developed over the years, and where that could take her. With her experience on the boards of VicHealth, Very Special Kids and the Murdoch Children's Research Institute, along with her highly developed skills in stakeholder engagement, reputation management and social media, 'It seemed madness not to take the opportunity and use the skills I've got in a different way.'

She was still focusing on the business but talking to one or two people in her network, and very quickly she was invited onto three new boards in just six months. As this experience has grown — Jane now has directorships with a private sector board, a government board, and a not-for-profit board — she is coming to an understanding of the nuances involved in this work, and has firm views on its implications and the importance of being honest with yourself by recognising what you can offer and why you want to offer it.

Being asked to join boards is an exciting and heady experience, particularly if you're used to consulting and you like new things, new ways of thinking, and get bored easily. Having all these new experiences, people, environments, what more could Jane ask for? Jane firmly believes that these appointments bring with them an obligation to be the best she can be, and it is important that she offers and develops the right attributes and skill set to be a highly effective non-executive director. So, despite her recognised experience in the health and not-for-profit sectors, Jane completed the Australian Institute of Company Directors course.

Many people speculate whether experience on not-for-profit boards is an important stepping stone to an appointment on a for-profit or ASX-listed board. Jane believes the experience and issues not-for-profit boards deal with are different, and can actually be much more complex. For example, the split between governance and management on not-for-profit boards is more tenuous and complex, often requiring directors to implement decisions that would strictly fall within a management domain — simply because community organisations don't have the resources, skills or staff to implement major decisions themselves. There is often an expectation from the small cause-driven organisations that directors will do a lot more than fulfil typical directorial responsibilities. The reality with not-for-profit boards, Jane believes, is that they usually invite people on least of all because of their governance skills, and more likely because they possess a professional skill that is needed such as communications advice, legal or financial advice. She herself does not sit on an ASX-listed board and does not think her experience will take her in that direction; however, she has and does sit on government and private-sector boards. On these boards, the delineation between management responsibility and board responsibility is much clearer. In fact, the more sophisticated the board, the clearer that split is, and in Jane's view it's much easier to be a director on the more sophisticated boards where these roles are clear.

Jane's advice to individuals seeking a board directorship is to identify a board where they actually want to make a difference around that table. It is clear to everyone when somebody is only involved because they want a career-enhancing move, not because they care. However, Jane contends that if you select a board you care about, and if you do it well, you will meet people, gain a reputation, and get opportunities that could well enhance your career prospects — but it is the integrity of the intention to serve on a board that will make this happen.

'What would I tell my younger self?'

'You can't control everything, but if you're out there and you're interested and you're engaged, great opportunities come up.'

'I am very sympathetic towards those who don't have choices, but most of us do have choices; have courage and take some of them.' Most choices, in Jane's experience, come around as a result of happenstance — a confluence of events that suddenly come together to present an opportunity — and these opportunities should be taken up and relished.

Taking up opportunities was what led Jane to move to Australia, set up her first business with Max, join the board of

Very Special Kids, and do numerous other things in her career. None of these were planned, but all of them proved fruitful or enjoyable in some way.

'I wasn't meant to end up at Very Special Kids. It happened, it was something that came my way, and I took it. It was that exposure outside, and then you meet people, and if you meet people opportunity happens. I'm a great believer in being in the right place at the right time, and I wish I could say it's all planned.'

Annwyn Godwin
A Public–Private Partnership

Annwyn Godwin, Merit Protection Commissioner, is a rare breed of public sector senior executives, with a career that has skipped back and forth between the private sector and government, and across many worlds. Annwyn grew up in rural Victoria, had a taste of an elite private girl's school, and held her own in the man's world of the Australian Stock Exchange before returning to government. Her diverse background means she can relate to others on many levels and contribute a range of perspectives to government policy. Annwyn fits her career around family these days, but it wasn't always that easy.

Major Turning Points

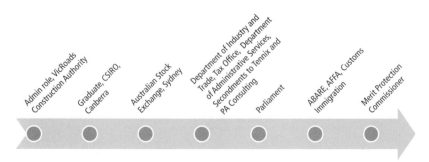

Admin role, VicRoads Construction Authority

Graduate, CSIRO, Canberra

Australian Stock Exchange, Sydney

Department of Industry and Trade, Tax Office, Department of Administrative Services, Secondments to Tennix and PA Consulting

Parliament

ABARE, AFFA, Customs Immigration

Merit Protection Commissioner

When we speak about careers and family, our words often stray into clichés or well-worn phrases such as 'achieving a balance between work and family', 'family-friendly practices' and 'having it all'. But the hope of many women to truly have it all — a successful career, a happy and fulfilling family life, and strong personal relationships — remains as elusive as ever. Instead, the words 'compromise', 'sacrifice' and 'adaptation' start to creep into our language and work–life balance is something that is out of reach until later in women's careers, if at all.

Annwyn's story is one about the commitment, compromise, sacrifice and love it takes to stay together as a family while both partners pursue their own demanding careers.

The public sector: leading the charge

The public sector in Australia has a long history of embracing equal opportunity for women and has led the way by introducing policies that enabled the implementation of flexible working practices.[1] In the 1970s, legislative groundwork was put in place with the Equal Employment Opportunity (EEO) in 1975 and the establishment of women's policy units in departments in 1976. By the 1980s, EEO programs had commenced, parental leave without pay was granted, permanent part-time work was introduced, and the first Senior Women in Management Program was introduced. In the 1990s, the *Workplace Relations Act* removed many restrictions imposed through awards and agreements for permanent part-time opportunities and more flexible arrangements were introduced such as broadband classifications, flexible work conditions and pay ranges to tailor to needs. The new *Public Service Act* (1999) legislated values of fairness, equity and workplace diversity, and enshrined merit as the basis of Australian Public Service (APS) employment. The *Amended Public Service Act 2013* further reinforced these principles.

Some key milestones were achieved at the turn of the 21st century, with women outnumbering men in the public service for the first time in 2001, the appointment of the first female secretary of a department in 2002 (Helen Williams, Secretary of the Department of Education in 1985) and four women appointed as agency heads in 2004. By June 2011, women comprised just over 38 percent of the Senior Executive Service and 46 percent of executive-level and feeder-group employees. Contrast this with the ASX 500 companies, where only 9.2 percent of senior executive positions are held by women.[2]

For the first time in Australia's history, women occupy two of the most powerful positions in Australian government (at the time of writing): Quentin Bryce was appointed governor-general in 2008, and Julia Gillard was appointed prime minister in 2010. Every state except South Australia has had a woman premier or chief minister.

The public sector: an opportunity rather than a calling

'My husband and I had already agreed that we were going to move around and do what we wanted to do, and we would be complementary in our careers. That didn't always pan out, but it was a nice principle to have when you first got married. I grew up with all of those beliefs that women can have it all. The whole thing for me was that, yes, of course you could have a career, and you could have a family, and you could be a wife and mother, and at the same time.'

Annwyn joined VicRoads around 1984–85 and the federal public service (CSIRO) in 1985–86 in the midst of the introduction of flexible working arrangements, not because she saw herself as a career public servant, or because of the flexible working arrangements on offer, but because it was the first job she was offered after graduating. She had friends in the Victorian Road Construction Authority who encouraged her to apply, so she took the opportunity. As she was married to an army officer at 21, working in the public service also meant she had more opportunities to relocate and find work when needed based on her husband's location.

> *'The public service was really good because my husband was in the army, so when he moved, or I moved, we eventually would catch up with each other in a particular city, as long as we stayed in the Canberra–Sydney–Melbourne triangle.'*

Despite equal opportunity enshrined in legislation, and flexible working policies and practices in place in the 1980s and 1990s, Annwyn's first experiences at the Victorian Road Construction Authority were not exactly positive. Annwyn recalls the double whammy: she was a woman *and* had married an army officer. Her manager's response, once he found out, was: 'It's bad enough you're female, because you'll go off and get pregnant, but the fact you've married an army officer means you're not going to stay here at all.' For many years, she didn't use her married name or wear wedding rings, as a direct result of that attitude. She didn't talk about her personal life. Her employers did not get the 'whole person' from her after that for many years.

While not denying that being an 'army wife' meant she would have to relocate frequently if she wished to be with her husband, her argument back to her manager, was: 'Men leave to do gap years, go back to study and travel overseas, so they're just as likely to leave as I am.'

Indeed, being a public servant meant that as long as she stayed in the triangle of Canberra, Sydney and Melbourne, she would be close to her husband's postings; however, being in the same city at the same time may be delayed. Together, at the start of their marriage, they pledged they would be complementary to each other's careers. This was a rather naïve but well-meaning principle, as Annwyn was to discover. Annwyn had grown up with the belief that women can have it all — a career and a family, being a wife and mother. This belief was tested and finally abandoned, as we shall read later.

So, what influenced Annwyn to become the strong, principled woman she is today? Like many of us, we need to rewind her story back to her childhood.

Finding her place

Annwyn was born in Benalla and grew up in Bendigo. One of three children, her parents were both professionals. Her father was an engineer and her mother had somewhat of a unique career working in Fiji in a secretarial role to the Office of the Governor-General and later as a private secretary to a solicitor in Suva. They always expected their children to go to university. There was a very strong sense of having to earn your place and provide value for money in whatever you did. Her parents had worked hard to give their children the opportunity of going to university. She remembers her father saying, 'We're giving you the opportunities that we didn't have, and we expect you to grab hold of those with two hands and go and do something with them.' These high expectations were reinforced externally by another person: Annwyn's grade four teacher, Janet Hollens, who saw a spark in her and one or two other children and gave them opportunities to try different things.

'When I reflect on it now, she was actually quite influential to me by saying, "It's okay to be different."'

These family expectations may have seemed rather odd in country Victoria in the '60s and '70s, when Annwyn's school friends were more likely to leave school at 16, get married and have children, or work on the farm, than complete year 12 or pursue tertiary studies. Being smart was not cool in that environment, and if you were too clever you stood out from the crowd.

Annwyn's break from Bendigo came with an overseas exchange program to share one year with the Workman family in Plainwell, Michigan, which opened her eyes to a world beyond the local community — so much so that she found it difficult to settle back into her local high school when she returned. Then came the lucky break that turned her life around. She received a supporting scholarship to attend Methodist Ladies College (MLC) in Melbourne for years 11 and 12. The teachers and students at MLC probably little imagined the impact these two years would have on Annwyn. Suddenly she found she fitted in — it was no longer socially difficult to be someone who was smart and an achiever. She blossomed. She was captain of the debating team and she represented the school at all sorts of public speaking engagements — opportunities she would never have received in Bendigo.

> 'When I went to MLC, it was a real relief in some ways. Suddenly I found people who thought like I did, and who were prepared to give things a go. I thought, "Wow, I'm not odd." I got really involved with the school and tried to take hold of the opportunities offered to me.'

Lessons learned from the Country Women's Association

Before her years at MLC, Annwyn's early view of the role of women was already strongly influenced by her childhood experiences with the Country Women's Association (CWA). These women were strong, courageous and resilient in times of adversity, and had the wisdom to see situations in a long-term context. One of her most striking memories of growing up around a farming community was during a period of terrible drought when Mary Harrison from the CWA kept saying, 'It's okay, the rain will come, the rain will come.' She and others were really asking the community to stick together and stay positive by recognising the cycle of life and keeping an eye on the long term. This was an attitude that strong, resilient women with fortitude, like the CWA women, taught Annwyn.

Another strong CWA memory is of a debutante's ball, which Annwyn recalls in great detail. 'We used to go out and help on the farm. This day we'd been helping the men who were shooting their livestock and their livelihood because of the terrible drought. We kids were picking up and moving the carcasses. Then that evening we all came in and had the most amazing night of dancing, in the local community hall, which was a Second World War Memorial building. While the men were out doing this, and us kids were helping them, the women had done this magnificent spread, a CWA spread of green jelly trifles and scones and cucumber sandwiches. We all got up and we had a wonderful night of dancing in the hall, which was arranged by the CWA for the next generation, and that's what I reflect on now. We've had an absolutely tough day but they wanted to show that this is for the next generation and that the terrible events of the day were actually not about us. They are about the cycle of life, staying positive and looking to the future. I get a shiver up and down my spine when I think of these memories.'

When she's going through a difficult time, Annwyn often thinks back to those CWA experiences and the lessons she learned about sticking it out through the tough times, because they will pass — they are part of a longer-term cycle. She will say to herself, 'This is more than just me; there's a much bigger picture here. If those men and those women can do that, then, jeez, what have I got to complain about?'

Annwyn's country upbringing, redolent with community, family, fairness and adversity, has left her with other important perspectives. She returns to the bush for walking and trekking to remind her of what is core during times of stress and being overworked. Here, she can recognise the time of day and the changing seasons, unlike during long days in the office, and those who have had an influence on her life. To the women of the CWA can be added many other earlier mentors, both on the farm such as Noel, Mary's husband, and in the office, such as Barry Lukeman from PA Consulting and Cameron (Ron) Hawthorne from the ASX.

Navigating through the Bermuda Triangle

After getting married, Annwyn applied for a graduate position at the CSIRO in Canberra, recognising that the Victorian Road Construction Authority was not for her and that her husband, Tony, would eventually get a posting to Canberra. She had witnessed other women being 'streamed' into stereotypical female roles — HR and corporate — while her male counterparts moved to roles in the harder-edged parts of the organisation. She had to push strongly to be moved out to a science program at the Department of Plant Industry, on Black Mountain, as close as she could get to a harder-edge part of the business. She later moved to Sydney with CSIRO, this time to work at the Australian Nuclear Science and Technology Organisation and catch up with her husband, who was now located there. This was an opportunity but she still did not necessarily see a long-term future in being a public servant.

After taking a redundancy package when the CSIRO was downsizing, the next turning point in her career was at the Australian Graduate School of Management, where she completed a Master's degree in Business Administration (MBA). From here, her public sector background, coupled with being a woman, enabled her to launch into the private sector. The Australian Stock Exchange was looking for an EEO project officer to develop and implement EEO policies. They assumed that as she came from the public sector she would know about 'this stuff'. Annwyn took the role and stayed with the ASX for several years, even after her husband returned to Canberra. She was discovered by an 'old, wise head gentleman, Ron', who recognised her potential and took her under his wing. He provided her with some amazing opportunities and mentored her for several years. After successfully completing a relatively small project, she was thrust into the heady world of establishing a national ASX body from a federation of state-based bodies. She was responsible for analysing the financial and industrial relations systems and policies of all of the different stock exchanges around Australia to determine how to mould them into one body.

'Ron said to me, "You've done a great job, a terrific job, you've understood the environment. Here, I've got some other work for you to do, do you want to stay on?" Of course I said yes.'

Ron's appointment of a young MBA with minimal financial background to this role took courage. Yet, to a large extent, Annwyn attributes her youth to her success. She was young and fresh, did not come with an accounting background or particular mindset, and did not have an agenda, so people were prepared to talk to her. Of course, Ron's support also helped, both in terms of giving her confidence and giving her authority. 'He'd send me off to meetings, and I would think, "What am I doing here?" He would say, "Just go, you have this intuition, just go with it and work with it, and see how you go. Talk to the people and just get them through this acquisition. I'll come in if I need to."' Ultimately, though, he believed in her ability, gave her the confidence and then pushed her out the door.

Where the dream ends and reality strikes

Even though they were married in 1984, Annwyn and her husband had not really lived as a married couple for the first six years of their marriage. Her husband would be called out on exercises to remote areas for three months at a time where he was not contactable, even by phone. At this time, the army were not actually supportive of couples where both partners worked (although their approach has changed since). Most wives stayed at home and supported their husbands, and the concept of finding work for a wife when the husband relocated was a foreign concept in those days. There were many instances where the army just did not understand the situation they were in. For instance, when Tony was offered a position in Tamworth and Darwin, there was no understanding that they would lose half their income if they both moved, as Annwyn would have to quit her job. Other army families with wives who stayed at home simply moved, with relatively minimal financial impact (although with the same social upheaval). In reality, her husband's career was probably more harmed by not accepting postings for his wife, than the short term impact on her career.

Coupled with commuting from Sydney to Canberra for several years, the point came where Annwyn had had enough. She and Tony had to decide if they were going to operate as a married couple or not. Annwyn had come to the realisation that those early dreams about having it all — the career, the family, and the relationship — were naïve and not sustainable in the long term. It simply became impossible for both of them to have two full-time careers, have a family and maintain the lifestyle they wanted. She had to make choices, and it wasn't just about her; it was about what was happening with her family and her husband's career. This was a time of soul-searching, for reflecting on her values and what was important to her.

'It was naïve to think that you could have everything all the time, and that there weren't any compromises that you'd ever have to make. I think there were a few stark moments, when it was a case of making a call, what actually is more important to you? Is your relationship more important than your career, or vice versa, and how is that going to pan out?'

This period culminated in Annwyn's decision to move out of her 'perfect role' at the ASX and back to Canberra — first to the Department of Industry and Trade, then to the Australian Taxation Office. Soon after, she and Tony started a family. Annwyn did not take naturally to the role of being a mother with a tiny baby. The first year or so of babyhood and motherhood was hard going for her, especially as her family were all back in Melbourne and her husband would be away for extended periods of time. So, after six months of maternity leave, she returned to work part-time, also driven in part by the unavailability of childcare to enable full-time work. Going back to work was when her 'super-mum' persona came into play. 'What I found when I came back part-time was that I had these expectations of myself of being a full-time mother, a full-time wife, and a full-time office worker. I put incredible pressures on myself as a part-timer, and that wasn't sustainable.' As soon as she put her son into full-time childcare, that pressure eased and she no longer had that expectation that she could (or should) do everything.

After the birth of her second child, Annwyn took a full year of maternity leave, thinking, 'Maybe I didn't give this motherhood thing a good-enough go.' She experienced post-natal depression and came to the realisation that being a full-time mother was not an option for her. When the last two children came along, her husband took a combination of long service leave and annual leave to care for them so Annwyn could return to work as soon as possible. Today, she has four beautiful children whom she loves dearly, the last two born when she was in the Senior Executive Service (SES), and is reaping the joys of motherhood with older children.

Annwyn believes her children have made her a much better manager and give her much-needed balance in her life. No-one was going to stop her from legitimately meeting the needs of her children, whether it be to attend an event or just be home at a reasonable time, and this ensures she does not spend extraordinary hours in the office.

Annwyn experienced very different reactions at work when she was in the SES and had her last two children — it was fine to have children and work part-time if you were in a middle management role but not quite as acceptable if you were in the SES. It seemed the stereotypes of where a woman belongs were still at play, with some managers believing she couldn't be serious about her career if she took time out to have a family.

> *'You were damned if you did and damned if you didn't. If you didn't take time off to spend with your children, then you heard, "Oh, she must be a terrible mother," and if you did take time off work then you weren't serious about your career.'*

However, we have gone ahead in the story — back to Annwyn's time in Canberra in the 1990s and as a mother of four children.

On-again, off-again relationship

It was time for Annwyn to take control of her career direction. She read the tea leaves and decided outsourcing was going to be important in the future. She decided controversially to move from her role in Tax to the Department of Administrative Services (DAS) — what she describes as moving from a 'sexy role' to a 'non-sexy area' to develop these new skills in outsourcing. What really appealed to Annwyn was the on-again, off-again 'affair' she was having with the private sector. While at DAS, she was appointed to the Executive Development Scheme and experienced three five-month secondments to work with a range of private sector companies including Ernst & Young and PA Consulting, and through them the engineering firm Tenix and Blake Dawson Waldron. Her strategy was to develop good networks to enable her to return to the private sector, which seemed likely. She loved working for these firms; there were clear goals and outcomes, stretching work and clear rewards for good performance. The private sector was open to new ideas and taking up business opportunities as they arose, and allocating resources to implement good ideas, provided there was a sound business case. Although it was tougher to achieve results, the rewards and the recognition were there.

Yet going back to the private sector a second time was a useful lesson for Annwyn. She was able to contrast the rewards of both sectors and reflect on the values instilled in her by her family and the CWA women about the importance of community and long-term sustainability. The public sector won out when she realised it aligned with her value system. This was a pivotal moment that changed the course of Annwyn's career. There was this sudden leap of understanding when it came to her what her life's career would be. Up to this point she was a public servant because it was comfortable to be a public servant, rather than because it was her calling. Now, it all changed and there was a conscious decision at that point to dedicate herself to the public sector. Annwyn described the way she felt about this decision as: 'Wow, I actually want to do this. I'm no longer going to be reliant on just doing a job in the public service. This is actually where I want to be, and where I need to be, and I want to make a real difference and … to be in a position to influence policy.' From this point onwards, she realised she had to step up to the SES and all that it entailed.

Annwyn also experienced a shift in her thinking about rewards for performance. The public sector has a different set of rewards that are not financially based. For instance, Annwyn's proudest moments today are when she represents Australia overseas — you can't put a price on that buzz. Other rewards that Annwyn values highly are the flexibility and the autonomy to be in control of her time and her priorities rather than being at the control of a client.

By this, she means she can take a long-term view on issues rather than a short-term perspective based around cash flow, which was Annwyn's experience in the private sector.

Her experience in the private sector, especially around negotiating contracts, meant she was moved around in the Department of Agriculture, Fisheries and Forestry (Australia) (AFFA), negotiating service-level agreements or resolving contracts that had gone pear-shaped', including a time in the Australian Bureau of Agricultural Resource Economics (ABARE), mainstream AFFA in HR and on to Customs and Immigration. Finally, she was appointed to her current role as Merit Protection Commissioner. She was encouraged to apply for this role by the departing Merit Protection Commissioner because she had expressed strong views about how things could be done better and how the function could be improved. He challenged her to step up and be counted. This role undertakes independent external reviews of employment actions affecting APS employees, ensuring agencies meet their obligations under the APS Values and Code of Conduct and that individual employees are given a 'fair go' in the employment decisions that affect them.

Throughout Annwyn's career she deliberately chose not to participate in women's specific programs such as the Senior Women in Management (SWIM) Program. While she recognises the value of women having access to these types of programs, she chose to participate in the Executive Development Scheme with both men and women instead, because she wanted to succeed in what she considered to be an equal playing field and did not want the risk of being marginalised by women's only programs.

Her choice has always been to be open to possibilities and to push the boundaries of her professional roles. This has meant that in the private sector she has worked in the extremes of submarines and office towers, been rewarded for being innovative and creative and rejected for being too young and naïve. In the public sector, she's done some weird and wonderful things such as assessed housing on Thursday Island, searched cargo ships for giant African snails, been lost in Parliament House, cared for trainee sniffer dogs, got bogged in sand dunes in Western Australia, and eaten witchetty grubs as part of a cultural interchange, through to representing Australia in international forums.

> 'All these experiences grow me and my mosaic is still evolving as I am. From my work titles it is not immediately obvious that these experiences could have been possible and yet by being open to possibilities, they have.'

Lessons for her younger self

Reflecting back on her career, Annwyn has five key messages she would tell her younger self:

- *Lesson #1*: Don't be so naïve to think that there won't be compromises in life. There will be compromises in life, but understand what is dear to you and don't compromise those things. On everything else, be flexible and open to other ways and ideas — yours is not always the right way.

- *Lesson #2*: Be bold — take more risks and don't be afraid to ask or stand up for what you believe. Don't question your worth, and ask for opportunities or exposure to new experiences.

- *Lesson #3*: Take time out for reflection and try to recognise your choices or decisions. Often, the small and insignificant ones cumulatively set us along paths and adventures we could never have planned. Whether they be bland or vibrant choices, polished or roughly hewed decisions, they are all part of your mosaic of life.

- *Lesson #4*: Do your due diligence on the manager you will be working for, not just the job. This person must have integrity and honesty, must have some political savvy and enough influence to get the resources they need for their agency. They must be approachable and treat everyone, including junior staff, with respect.

- *Lesson #5*: Be open to possibilities in your professional roles and always try to see an issue from a number of perspectives. This will open doors to opportunities and experiences that may not otherwise be part of your job or even have been possible.

Annwyn has just been reappointed Merit Protection Commissioner for another five years — another first as Commissioner. That will be 10 years in one role, the longest time she has ever spent in one place, yet she still feels energised and enthusiastic about the challenges facing her: 'No day is ever the same.' One can only wonder what lessons this period will hold for her.

REFLECTIONS AND CONCLUSIONS

Catherine Nance

The Future of Work: A Woman's Perspective

Catherine Nance is a partner and actuary at PricewaterhouseCoopers (PwC), where she heads the National Retirement Incomes and Asset actuarial consulting group. Catherine has over 20 years' professional experience advising governments, companies and superannuation funds in superannuation, employee benefits, investment consulting, aged care, and finance and investment-related work.

She is currently a Director, and a Chair of the Audit Committee, of the Western Australian Treasury Corporation and a Director of the Government Employees Superannuation Board of WA. She was previously a Director of Community CPS Australia Limited.

Catherine's charming and approachable manner is what first strikes you when you meet her. Yet, as soon as she speaks, Catherine commands immediate respect and you can understand how she became one of the rare group of senior partners in professional services firms based in Melbourne.

Since 2004, when she was appointed as one of the first generation of women partners at PwC in Perth, Catherine Nance has had considerable experience in assessing the performance of businesses and in developing ways to improve the way they work and to create value.

Our conversation started with her view, from an actuarial perspective, of the future of work for women. It was a rich conversation, interspersed with stories and anecdotes from her own personal journey. This chapter is somewhat more a discussion of her perspectives, supported with some excellent data, than a discussion of her career at an individual level.

Some figures: 21st-century women at work

A comparison of research from the United States and from Australia reveals some interesting facts.

Hanna Rosin, in her book *The End of Men*,[1] claims that the US is, or soon will be, living under a matriarchy. She concludes that 'the US economy is in some ways becoming a kind of travelling sisterhood':

- In 2009, American women outnumbered men in the workforce for the first time.
- They now outnumber men on degree courses by a ratio of three-to-two, and are even beginning to 'crowd out men' in science and engineering courses.
- More and more families depend on the woman as the main breadwinner (almost 64 percent in Washington, DC).
- Of the 15 most expanding job categories in the US, 12 are now dominated by women.

The Australian economy, by contrast, has not reached these startling statistics. Yet perhaps we are not so far off. For instance:

- As at October 2012, women comprise 35 percent of the workforce.[2]

- In August 2011, 59 percent of women were in the labour force, and their participation rate is steadily increasing each year. By contrast, 82 percent of men were in the labour force and their participation rate has been declining.[3]

- Women graduates have outnumbered men on degree courses since the 1980s (a steady 51 percent of women were graduates from 1988 to 1992).[4] By 2011, 57 percent of higher education students were women.[5]

- In 2011, women outnumbered men two-to-one in management and commerce degrees.[6]

- Eighty percent of purchases or purchasing decisions are made by women.[7]

- Women live longer than men. A boy born in 2009 to 2011 can expect to live to almost 80 years, while a girl can expect to live just over 84 years.[8]

Enabling women to succeed in the workplace, however, seems to be a continual challenge. Despite the fact that more women undergraduates are entering the workforce than men:

- Only six percent of line management positions in the ASX 200 are held by women (the pipeline to many CEO roles).

- There are only seven female CEOs in the ASX 200 (up from six in 2010).

- Women still hold only 12 percent of ASX 200 directorships and only 9.7 percent of executive roles.

- Fifty-six percent of ASX 500 companies still do not have a woman on their boards.[9]
- Australia is ranked 50th in the world for women's workforce participation relative to men's.[10]

These figures have shifted in the last couple of decades, but at a glacial pace. In 1994, women represented only three percent of all board members, one percent of executive directors and four percent of non-executive directors. There has been no increase in the number of women on boards in the previous three years.[11]

The public sector seems to have fared somewhat better:

- In Australia, at the time of writing, we currently have a woman prime minister, governor-general and speaker in Parliament.
- For over 20 years, we have had women premiers in every state and territory in Australia except South Australia.
- In 2012, women made up 24.7 percent of elected positions in the House of Representatives and 38.2 percent of the senate.[12]
- At June 2011, women comprised 57.5 percent of all Australian Public Service employees[13] and held 35.3 percent of government board appointments, with four government portfolios meeting the gender-balance target.[14]

Yet despite these figures, Australia remains ranked 41st in the world for women in ministerial positions.[15]

What's more, the *Global Gender Gap Index* shows Australia dropped eight rankings between 2006 and 2011 from 15th to 23rd,[16] indicating that Australia is regressing compared to other nations in closing the gender gap.

'How is our workforce developing, and what will it look like in the foreseeable future?'

The weight of numbers

*'I think ageism will have to vanish through sheer weight of numbers.
I think that discrimination towards women will also vanish.'*

First, the workforce will continue to age. The 55+ age group
is a significant and essential component of the labour market,
representing 15 percent of the total workforce in Australia.[17] There
is also a cohort of workers aged 45–54 that are moving through and
will provide the fastest-growing labour market segment in the next
decade.[18] By the year 2016, it is estimated that in New South Wales
alone there will be more people over 65 years of age than people 15
years and under.[19]

Secondly, the participation of women in the Australian labour
force is expected to grow. IBISWorld, an independent market
research company, expects the participation of women to grow by
2.7 percent over 2013–14, to reach 5.79 million females, outpacing
growth in the male workforce and closing the gender gap.[20]

A report by Deloitte, prepared on behalf of the Australian Human
Rights Commission, uncovered three factors that would impact on
workforce participation in Australia in the foreseeable future:

1. Higher participation rates among women.

2. Increases in the age pension requirement, with the age for
   women increasing to 65.5 by mid-2017, followed by the age for
   both women and men rising to 67 by mid-2023. increasing the
   participation of older workers in the labour market.

3. Shifts in traditional attitudes to retirement, as Australians
   adjust to significant increases in longevity.[21]

The natural outcome in having an ageing population with
women outliving men is that workforce participation rates will

continue to increase in the over-55s, with an increasing proportion of the workforce comprising women.

This raises two interesting questions. First, does this trend mean equality in the workforce will be driven purely by the force of numbers? Secondly, what difference will these changes make to the profile of executives holding leadership positions?

While the force of numbers is a factor in promoting equality, our ability to achieve it will be too slow without positive intervention, argues Catherine. Intervention is essential to circumvent a number of stereotypes and biases that, firstly, confound our ability to achieve equality and, secondly, restrict access to powerful leadership positions. 'Before you get change, usually you have to have a very active period of hustling for change,' she has observed. In Australia, the issue of imposing quotas on companies is again being debated, as are other strategies such as voluntary targets. This is because relying on the greater participation of women in the workforce (i.e. on demographic pressures alone) hasn't had much impact in the effort to build equality of opportunity.

Laura Liswood, author of *The Loudest Duck*, agrees that the numbers game alone does not lead to greater diversity. She argues that you need to shape attitudes at all organisational levels, and foster a fair and equal working environment, and that the way to do this is by eliminating subtle advantages and disadvantages to specific groups.[22]

Ageism

'Once we've all slipped towards the 50 and over [age bracket], we're sort of slipping off the radar.'

Catherine believes that business's view of ageism — that older workers are somehow less productive, less energetic, less competent and have fewer ideas than younger generations — must change. Catherine recounts a story of a workplace that introduced a new program encouraging staff to think laterally, be innovative and develop out-of-the-box solutions. However, this program was only available to young graduates aged in their 20s because it did not occur to management that older employees might want or could contribute to this program. These types of programs perpetuate the myths about older workers lacking ideas or initiative. Yet there is a growing body of research that demolishes these stereotypical biases. For instance:

- Lockheed Martin, an American global aerospace, defence, security and advanced technology company, were able to demonstrate that the costs associated with retaining older workers, including retraining and the redesign of jobs, tools and practices, can be offset through improved performance, lower claims and reduced medical costs. Retaining older workers is also likely to assist in the transmission of highly desirable work traits, such as loyalty and a strong work ethic, from older to younger workers.[23] Older employees are also often custodians of a large amount of corporate knowledge and have strong industry networks, both highly valuable to employers and difficult to replicate in younger employees.

- Research conducted in the US in 2010 found that the greatest productivity loss occurs in employees aged in their 30s, whereas productivity loss occurs *least* in employees aged 60 or older.[24]

- Other research into Nobel Prize winners and great inventors found that innovators are around six years older today than they were a century ago. This shift, the researchers concluded, is consistent with the life-cycle productivity of great minds (this increases as they get older) and is also consistent with an ageing workforce.[25]

- Finally, the average founder of a high-tech startup isn't a whiz-kid graduate, but a mature 40-year-old. Older entrepreneurs have higher success rates when they start companies and the highest rate of entrepreneurship in America has shifted to the 55–64 age group, with people over 55 almost twice as likely to found successful companies than those between 20 and 34.[26]

These stereotypes are not just perpetuating inequity. There is an increasing body of research that demonstrates they also have real implications for business performance, productivity and the health of the economy. Research shows that:

- Australia, and indeed many countries worldwide, are facing talent shortages, which will only worsen. We will need older people to work because we won't have enough workers otherwise.

- McKinsey reported that, by 2040, Europe will have a shortfall of 24 million workers aged 15 to 65. This gap can be reduced to three million if the proportion of women in the workplace was raised to that of men.[27]

- In Australia, the retirement of many baby boomers born in 1946 to 1954 will probably mean that companies are going to lose large numbers of senior-level employees in a short period of time; in the US, nearly one-fifth of the working-age population (16 and older) will be at least 65, with a big proportion retired, by 2016.

- Deloitte Access Economics sees the expected increases in the participation of older workers producing a $55 billion or 2.7 percent increase in national income by 2024–25. This report predicts that a five percent increase in participation by older workers would contribute an extra $48 billion in GDP or 2.4 percent of national income.[28]

- A Goldman Sachs report found that closing the pay gap between men and women alone would boost Australia's GDP by 11 percent.[29]

Catherine is optimistic about the impact of the economic forces of demand and supply of older workers.

'At the moment there's neither demand nor supply. Companies don't want them, and they don't want to work; they're still in this old mix of having a goal to retire at 60.'

The demographic shifts discussed above will drive a fundamental change in thinking and behaviour. People in their 50s and over will want to stay involved and active in the workforce, as the traditional retirement age of 60 or 65 will have less meaning when people live for another 20 or 30 years.

The changing nature of work

These demographic shifts are likely to create changes in the workplace or the work itself. In fact, Catherine sees some fundamental shifts already occurring in the nature of work and in the relationship between the employer and employee. Some of these shifts include:

- A dominant pattern of contract work and portfolio careers emerging. A portfolio might be six months' work for one company, six months' work for another. Or it might comprise layers of concurrent activities, such as directorships, consultancy, teaching, investing, community organisation involvement, etc.

- This emergence of contract work and portfolio careers for women may extend to senior positions, eliminating some of the obstacles to women reaching the top, and even opening up opportunities. As with all contract work, the disadvantages are that you are not part of a collective of employees. On the other hand, you will not be beholden to one employer.

- Measures such as employee engagement, employer brand or reputation and net promoter scores (a management tool used to gauge the loyalty of a firm's customer and internal relationships) will become less relevant for those engaged on a contract basis or will at least be redefined by the availability of flexible working conditions, contract opportunities and interesting work, rather than by culture and manager–employee relationships.

- Similarly, the concept of an *employee* will become less relevant as people build careers on contract or portfolio work.

Older workers can drive change

'We actually really need to encourage women and older people, 45s and over, to stay working, so why don't we start focusing on what they want, and drop some of the focus on Gen X and Y. The focus has been 99 percent on youth, nothing on anyone over 45.'

Older employees will have started to demand portfolio careers, flexible hours and part-time work as a smooth transition into a later retirement phase; however, the younger generation of workers find this appealing, too. AMP's findings into the retirement and superannuation practices of Australians[30] found that a gradual or incremental approach to retirement is becoming popular among older workers. In the five years prior to retirement age (60–64), 15 percent of men and 14 percent of women are in part-time employment. Further, in the 50–69 age group, of those people who changed their employment status, more of them changed to part-time work (nine percent) than to retirement (seven percent).[31] For many older workers, flexible work is specifically about phasing into retirement: over 40 percent of full-time workers, or around one million Australians, intend to switch to part-time work for a few years before retirement.[32] Younger employees may not feel like they've had the power to demand it, but if it's been negotiated by older workers and is on offer, they will take it.

What Catherine finds fascinating is that whatever organisations tend to do for the older employees seems to have incredible appeal for younger employees. Policy changes to do with flexible work practices, the introduction of mobile or home-based technology to enable flexible work arrangements, and the introduction of mentoring programs, for instance, are often targeted at, or driven by, older workers. But then the younger employees, such as Generation Y, see the benefits could also suit them, and they say, 'I really want that.' Then it will go right through the workplace.

Just as older workers can pave the way for younger workers, Catherine sees women driving changes that men will want access to, such as elder care and time off for children. Many men previously felt they could not demand time off for children, whereas now they are accessing these policies in far greater numbers. The 2011 ABS statistics indicate that 23 percent of men took advantage of parental leave policies. CEOs are beginning to lead the way through their own behaviour — it is no longer unusual for a male CEO to arrive at the office late after dropping off the children at school, or to leave early to attend children's events. This provides permission for others to adopt the same practices and behaviour.

Removing the bias

Catherine experienced gender bias only later in her career. There was no sense of male–female difference in her research career or in her earlier career as an actuary; as one of her previous employers said to her, 'An actuary is an actuary is an actuary.' There were enough women at conferences and in the office occupying a range of levels for gender to not be an issue.

Catherine encountered one situation where the first female in a group of 15 or so partners arrived a few minutes late for her first meeting, pulled up a chair and then found that they did not open up the circle to let her in. It was a symbolic moment!

She has also noted that it can be a struggle not promoting a man that other men want to promote. Sometimes it's easier for partners to hire a lateral recruit from another firm rather than choose between contenders within the organisation who each have alliances as colleagues or friends with one or other of the decision-making partners. (This may partly explain why some women get ahead by making lateral moves, such as many of the women profiled in this book, rather than waiting for an opportunity to be promoted up the ranks.)

Catherine has seen a marked positive change in the selection processes for promoting women in professional service firms over the past eight years. Implementing formal, more objective processes have minimised bias and ensured a more equal playing field. In partner assessment meetings in the past, Catherine recalls, 'You would get to the female, and one influential male would just make a comment like, "I don't think they really want it," and that would be enough to scuttle it.' Once a more formal process came into play, with robust and challenging conversations based on more objective, comparative metrics, women started making it through to partnership.

Today, women are made partners when they are pregnant. Now, they can take time off to have babies quite soon after being made partner, and they can work part-time and retain partner status. Some years ago, there would have been exclamations of 'How dare they!'

Self-selecting, or opening cracks

> 'The door has opened a crack for women but only in safe
> areas … they're in those lesser executive roles; they don't have
> the same power to exert the change needed.'

Women already self-select into industries, organisations or roles that are female-friendly. They have choices and exercise them. We see the rise of women entering small business, government, the tertiary sector, the community sector, health, and the services sector, where organisations tend to actually practice diversity, not just espouse it, and so have female role models in positions of influence. Many women decide that life in a big company is too difficult, and it doesn't accord with their values, so they choose to go where they can live their values.

Ticking the box on women in senior management is easy for companies when they can appoint women to support roles, or cost centres, or 'safe roles' — excluding them from what is perceived to be riskier operational, profit-centre roles, such as heads of businesses. Yet these 'profit-and-loss' roles comprise the pipeline to many future CEO and board roles, thereby placing another impediment in the way of women: that of mismatched experience for CEO or board roles.

The squeaky wheel

'I do think, at the moment, business favours the squeaky, demanding wheel, and I do think less women are naturally like that.'

At the risk of over-generalising, Catherine has observed that more women than men expect to be recognised, and don't *demand* to be recognised. If things don't go their way, rather than be confronting or demanding, they will put up with lack of recognition, decide this organisation isn't the right one for them and then they will they go somewhere else.

Laura Liswood aptly describes the squeaky — demanding — wheel syndrome and some contextual (or cultural) issues.[33] Liswood explores the unconscious beliefs people inherit from the world around them and the cultures in which they grow up. In the United States, for instance (and, Catherine would contend, in Australia), society teaches us that 'the squeaky wheel gets the grease' — implying that the loudest person gets the attention. In Chinese society, by contrast, 'the loudest duck gets shot'. Being outspoken in Western cultures is expected; in Chinese cultures, it is discouraged. Yet it is not as simple as this. If squeaky-wheel behaviour is broken down by gender, it seems to be more acceptable for a man to squeak than for a woman, in Western cultures at least. Cordelia Fine, in *Delusions of Gender*, reports a study by Laurie Rudman that showed what people found particularly objectionable in professional women was status-enhancing behaviours such as being aggressive, dominating and intimidating.[34] Fine observes the catch-22 situation for women: when they display confidence in their skills and comfort with power, they run the risk of being labelled 'competent but cold', with the only alternative to this perception being regarded as 'nice but incompetent'.[35]

Catherine has observed in professional services firms that this reluctance to be demanding means that women will often not publicly object to, or fight against, blockages to their professional advancement. Instead, many women who have not made what they consider a deserved partnership appointment will tend to move firms rather than stay and fight. Perhaps this anecdotally supports Fine and others' observations regarding status-enhancing behaviours and the pressure to conform to stereotypes.

This is not to suggest that women are not ambitious, but possibly they are ambitious in a different context than men, Catherine believes. Women are often ambitious about wanting to do a good job, wanting to be the best. On the other hand, men, while they are ambitious about wanting to do a good job, are often also ambitious about having the titles (and the power) as well. Catherine suggests there is something innate about women's ambition that they just don't want to be labelled as 'difficult' along the way and so take a lower profile and don't want to be seen as seeking power.

Lessons she would tell her younger self (and other women)

On mentoring programs

> 'One of the things that I realised quite early on with mentoring programs was that they can provide a good form of support, but there's no point being mentored by a woman if men are blocking progression. You need to be mentored by one of the men.'

On managing perceptions in the firm

'At times I have provided support to women trying to come up through the ranks, and they would say things like "I really don't know if I want it", "How do I juggle kids?", "How do I balance things; I don't know that I want to work those hours". So I'd say, "Tell that to me and get it out of your system, but never say that to those making the recruitment decisions. Let them offer the job to you, then you decide, but do not say that."'

On developing resilience

'I think, when women get knocked, sometimes they say, "It probably means that I'm just not good enough." I think that you've got to have an ability to say, "It is not personal; it is not saying that I'm not good enough." You've got to get up, dust yourself off, and demand what you want … what we don't do enough of is say what we want. It's very few women [who] will say, "I want to be made a partner, so what does it take to get me there?" They're worried that they're not good enough because, if they were, the firm should recognise them, and they wouldn't have to say it.

Women have to have more robustness about them. I think they've got to go for more opportunities. I think that they've got to have a little bit more robustness when they've taken a knock.'

On claiming what's yours

'Don't rely on informal or confidential promises such as, "It is too hard to appoint you as partner at this time. Over the next period do such and such, then we'll make you a partner." The prospective senior partner or sponsor who makes such

commitment could then be gone in six months, so then where
does that leave you? It might take you another couple of years
going through an assessment program, and even if you were
rated at the top they may decide not to make you partner.'

Catherine is no stranger to putting herself forward. Being
relatively unknown when she joined PwC, she knew she could
be passed over for partnership by others more well-known, and
she understood she would have to go after this appointment and
change their perception of her. So she said to the partners, 'Let me
come over and talk to you personally about what my business does,
so that you heard it from me, rather than hearing it from other
people that don't know what my business does.' She flew over to
Sydney, took them through her business, and they put her up that
night to be made partner. At the new partner dinner, they were
introducing all the new partners along the lines, 'So-and-so is from
Brisbane, really great in tax,' and, 'So-and-so is here.' When they
got to Catherine, they said, 'Cathy wasn't so much invited to join
the partnership, but kicked the door in.' She knew it was meant to
be a compliment but couldn't help thinking, 'Why did I have to
"kick the door in"?'

Heather Carmody
The Gloves are Off in the Diversity War

Heather is a Principal Consultant with the Nous Group and specialises in organisation design. Heather is also a member of the Monash University Council and of the Rhodes Scholarship Selection Committee (Victoria).

Heather was Executive Director of the Business Council of Australia (BCA)'s Council for Equal Opportunity for five years.

Talk is cheap

This chapter is about quotas, but it is also a broader conversation about diversity and cultural change. This is because quotas cannot be discussed in isolation from the broader issues of values, attitudes and behaviours that permeate workplaces.

But let's start with the vexed subject of quotas. This subject generates the same level of passionate argument that we saw when legislation was introduced in the 1970s and 1980s.[1]

At its simplest, the protagonists argue that progress for women at the top has been glacial and offers no comfort that any significant change will occur without employers' hands being forced. Quotas will therefore force much-needed action.

The antagonists argue that quotas will generate unintended, negative outcomes such as token female appointments, cynicism and resistance to systemic culture change.

My view is that both 'camps' are right. The fact is that we have hit the proverbial brick wall in Australia. The only workplaces that do better than average in promoting women into senior roles and with appointing women to operational roles are those that are run by women or by men whose values and business logic cause them to champion women's advancement in a deliberate and sustained way. This is the cadre who have the persistence and skills required to really understand the social and psychological dynamics in their organisations, and the problems of unconscious bias and stereotyping. They are also the ones prepared to change the systems and change the conversations about merit, who will lead by example, and take calculated risks.

So we're still reliant on role models and savvy champions, which confirms that we don't have a level playing field.

The problem is that too few of these leaders have emerged in the corporate world over the past decade, so their impact on overall statistics is low. I was out to dinner recently where the guests included a man who has been a CEO for 20 years in Australia and overseas and two other men who have been the chief HR officer in global companies for at least 20 years. They are deeply experienced people — big multinational companies are their game, and it was pretty interesting to drop the subject of quotas onto the table. I said about three words on it and they took it up with great gusto. I didn't have to push. What was absolutely stark about the discussion was that the two HR chiefs both said, at the same time, 'Can't get any traction on the subject of women or quotas at all. The executive suite is not interested, don't have to be interested, won't be interested.' So I said, 'If they're not interested in having them [women] at the top, are you at least filling the pipeline?' He said, 'No. Nope, not, not.' These are ASX 25 companies. The CEO said, 'It's hopeless. They're there [the women], and then they lose focus, and then they come back, but it's too late.' I was gobsmacked. So, for 20 years, we've talked about the labour market and the changing structural nature of the workforce with an ageing and shrinking talent pool. We've talked about the changing structure of the economy whereby the resources sector is where the revenue comes from, but the services sector is where the employment is — then you strike these beliefs and attitudes! It is as if the conversations we had over 30 years ago when I headed the BCA's Council for Equal Opportunity haven't moved on.

The mining, manufacturing and infrastructure companies where these men came from are not alone. This is an attitude that I have personally observed in the finance sector also. The economic argument for diversity is not uniformly compelling. Despite clear instructions from the CEO of one major bank to 'do something about it' (getting women into the senior ranks), the conversation still languishes around how to build the argument to get inside the heads and hearts of their peers who are convinced there is an endless supply of talent prepared to work 24/7. These men just don't seem to get it. Of course, this approach means many women will look elsewhere and achieving diversity targets will be as elusive as ever. It doesn't help that the finance sector will experience a tight business environment for several years ahead.

We used to believe that if you fill the pipeline, good things would happen eventually. Couple that with the changes in the workforce and the economy, and you could actually retain optimism — but for these beliefs and attitudes.

Godzilla meets Bambi

It would be incorrect to generalise about attitudes of all men at all levels and in all organisations; however, there seems to be a bifurcation when managers are elevated to senior roles in large corporations. It is like an occupational hazard: they achieve senior roles partly because of what it takes to get there, which is generally about demonstrating a 24/7 commitment, which often means subordinating the needs of family to the needs of the organisation. Once there, they often have a dependent spouse, if they've got a spouse, and have long since lost sight of what it's like to try and manage everything outside work; they've long since abandoned the idea of being a present parent, if they're a parent, or a very present son or daughter if they've got ageing parents.

I am more optimistic when observing how smaller businesses operate — which is where almost half the workforce is located, and which contributed over a third of production in 2009–2012.[2] For example, at Nous, many of our staff are active parents, male and female. Lots of them work from home regularly and come and go from the office. Many men and women of younger generations are deciding they don't want to work in some of the big companies, and they'll be part of the growth of small businesses. Overall, these are fantastic signals. However, none of them are running big organisations; they can't and they won't because they are not prepared to work to the 24/7 mantra demanded by most big businesses. Breakthrough changes are needed at the top end of town but will only happen if there is a perceived need. It is not immediately obvious where that will come from.

Let's discuss culture and change

Appointing women consistently to leadership positions is such a deep-seated cultural issue that nothing short of a transformation in culture is required, which takes years — years that many CEOs do not have because they don't usually stay in the CEO role long enough to drive sustainable change. In April 2012, Goldman Sachs Australia released a report entitled 'CEO Turnover: Implications of Declining Tenure and Longevity Risk'.[3] The report found the median ASX 100 CEO tenure is now only 3.9 years and decreasing (it was nine months longer five years ago). CEO turnover is also accelerating. Between 2003 and 2007, CEO turnover averaged only nine percent per year. In 2009, after the Global Financial Crisis (GFC), the rate spiked to 22 percent. The report goes on to say: 'In our view ... shorter CEO tenure is impacting decision-making, leading to insufficient regard for longer-term strategy, and discouraging long-term investment and value creation.'[4]

Culture is entrenched, both good and bad, so to successfully change culture, CEOs need to aggressively pursue change in their first year, building a critical mass of leaders and supporters of change prepared to think and act differently. It takes time to win over those employees who are not engaged with the proposed change or who actively dissociate from it. Ultimately, a CEO wants all employees to embrace the change, so needs to allow time for them to either get on board or eventually leave.

We can take heart, however, in reflecting on some great examples of success. Bob Joss, the Westpac chief hired in 1993 to save the bank after it posted the largest net loss in Australian corporate history, imposed much-needed management discipline and culture change by appointing women to senior positions to break down the blokey culture in the bank. Many of these women remain in key leadership positions today, including Ann Sherry, AO, one of the successful leaders profiled in this book. George Trumbull transformed AMP from a conservative, inward-looking organisation to an aggressive market competitor, using leadership diversity as a key lever. A succession of CEOs at Citibank have made great strides. Peter Shergold and Terry Moran, both secretaries of the Department of the Prime Minister and Cabinet (PMC), have long track records and strong reputations in supporting, developing and promoting women as part of their transformation strategies in the public sector.

Leading such change is not without its risks. Within any cohort of women, there will be successful and unsuccessful women, and women who are good at mentoring and supporting other women, and women who are not — just as not all appointments of men are successful. However, the biggest risk is appointing women as a form of tokenism. Some CEOs can be publicly positive about change and look like leaders, but if they put on their executive boards women who are not good at their job, or who are in roles that shouldn't be on the executive board, they are sending the wrong message. These CEOs are clearly making this change just for the numbers. A CEO has to be incredibly careful about merit and fair practice, and how it is perceived in an organisation. While the intent of quotas is to accelerate the embedment of fair practices in relation to the target group, it can backfire if the actual impact is to damage employees' perceptions of fairness or merit. Getting the numbers for numbers' sake is not the answer.

Looking further afield to countries that have imposed quotas, there is little evidence that they automatically elevate women into senior positions. Norway, for instance, has a quota of 40-percent women on boards. This may sound great, but if it is the same cohort of women who are being appointed to more boards, then there is minimal change in the actual numbers of women being given these opportunities. Sometimes it is easier to appoint women to boards than to place them in powerful leadership positions within corporations. Thus, quotas on boards do not necessarily translate into increased numbers of women into executive positions or pipeline roles to becoming a CEO.

The power of quotas could be in the threat of quotas

I've seen the issue from many perspectives. My experience includes establishing equal opportunity in organisations as an internal manager, consulting for endless numbers of organisations, and a role with a peak employer group. My own view is that the threat of quotas is very useful. The threat has been a factor in galvanising the Male Champions of Change (a group of leading CEOs/secretaries) into public commitments and leadership on women's advancement, and in director and employer groups taking decisive actions. It has also led to challenging and productive public debate.

There is a genuine fear of quotas among women as well as men. It is likely that there are few people who would be happy to be regarded as a token appointment. There is substantial evidence that quotas and targeted appointments can actually slow the rate of progress of systemic cultural change, which is what produces sustained improvement in women's employment.

There is strong anecdotal evidence that colleagues will assume someone appointed under a quota system is less capable. So, rightly or wrongly, quotas are commonly perceived to be unfair. As I indicated above, felt fairness is one of the most critical elements of a productive workplace and engaged workforce.

If not quotas, then what?

The most important approach needed in organisations that want to improve their performance is to tackle it like any other successful cultural change process. That means the CEO needs to build the business case for change and then lead the change process. The HR department is not the right owner. It also means — like any other change — targets need to be set, roadblocks removed, and monitoring and sanctions need to be robust.

The additional feature of well-designed culture change in this case is that in Australia it inevitably will involve a review of the leadership model in use. Understanding the nature of cultural fit and what behaviours and mindsets are in use (as distinct from the formal performance and capability criteria) is critical. This can be a very challenging piece of work. It generally defies the status quo and so will be resisted. Only the CEO can lead this work.

The research is unequivocal that successful managers must be defined more broadly than simply by their capacity to understand the numbers, make decisions and hit financial targets.

The requirement of managers needs to include, as a minimum, a capability to engage productively with stakeholders and staff and to motivate others. Once that has happened, the way is paved to re-value communications and the so-called softer skills. In turn, that opens up a broader cohort of candidates for managerial and board roles. Inevitably, it increases the pool of women, but my experience is that it also broadens the male pool.

Another important element of the management model is the message given about expectations or allowances regarding the number of hours worked, the place of work (office or home), and judgments about commitment and performance. Generally, women executives send different messages to staff about this than their male peers. For employees who have external commitments to juggle — primarily but not always women — these messages can be a game-changer in terms of their willingness to go for the senior jobs.

Targets are the hardwiring

The adage 'what gets measured gets managed' applies to this area of change like any other. However, the focus of these measures needs to be on managers — not women. In any other area of business measurement, managers of teams are held to account for their performance and the performance of their team. So it should be with their female appointments and promotion practices. It is no longer women who have to change. They've done their changing — got the degree, got the numbers, got the mentors and so on.

It is their managers, and the culture and HR practices these managers preside over, that have to change. Women are the new norm in our labour market, so managers who can't adapt their practices and style to reflect this are arguably not equipped for the job.

Why go to all this effort?

Hanna Rosin[5] and others offer an interesting angle on the 'it makes good business sense' argument. These writers articulate how significantly the world has changed. Woman-power has actually arrived, without any great fanfare. Aside from the well-known facts about women now holding the majority of undergraduate and postgraduate degrees and holding more tertiary qualifications than men, it is instructive to look at the structural economic changes going on in developed countries.

In the last US recession, three-quarters of the eight million jobs lost were held by men. The losses came from 'male' industries: high-end finance, construction and manufacturing. Women now hold the majority of jobs in the US. Most of the job growth in developed economies is coming from sectors dominated by women. This includes the personal service industry that caters primarily to women who are using their degrees at work and require domestic support and personal health and wellbeing services. This is the case in Australia, with the possible exception of resources — although the resources companies are aggressively and successfully increasing their female workforces.

The workforce of only 30 years ago that relied on physical strength is all but gone. It can be easily argued that men have been slower to adapt to these economic and social changes than women. Part of the adaptability of women along the way has been their willingness to make bold decisions about where and how they choose to work. Legions of women have left, particularly from big corporate organisations, when they found the attitudes, inflexibility and sometimes their business principles to be at odds with their own needs and values.

One of my early formative management experiences was establishing a 'greenfield' organisation in regional Victoria. It involved recruiting about 25 health professionals and administrators from a tight labour market. I competed by offering a myriad of working time arrangements and the promise of interesting work. It was a winning strategy.

Australia's unique culture

It seems that in Australia the challenge of supporting and encouraging women in leadership roles is somewhat more vexed than in other countries. We seem to be struggling more with this concept than some of our neighbouring countries. Perhaps this is due to the prevalence of some pervasive cultural norms in Australia, like women should be at home with their children. In my experience in New Zealand, working with the same cohort of CEOs and executives, the obstacles and the resistance is not as great. Also, look at the emerging economies in China and India. Their labour markets are much less segregated than in Australia. Further afield, the French have always been interesting. French women expect to have children and to not miss a beat with their careers.

> *If we don't deal with the occupational segregation women continue to experience in Australia, the rest of the world will just run right over us.*

Nevertheless, I am optimistic about the future of women in Australian business for many reasons. First, I believe the structural shift in the nature of the economy and the labour market towards a service economy is irreversible. And a service economy is really well suited to many women. Women will continue to be the engine room of small- and then middle-sized organisations, because they are well-educated, they are already in the service economy in large numbers and they're just better at it. I can see a future where the labour market will be segregated along a totally different dimension. It may look something like this: women as well as men will go into the big-name organisations because they'll want it for their CV, but women won't stay there if the company does not meet their needs. Women are smart and they will work their way through in an increasingly attractive economic structure, finding some way to operate in organisations that value them — whether that be government, small business or other opportunities. It is quite possible that these economic shifts will drive the diversity agenda, more than logic or sophisticated business cases.

Secondly, I have seen a number of the young women over the years make very deliberate decisions to move out of the private sector for four or five years while they bring a couple of children into the world, and then they'll go back and pick up where they left off in the private sector. If they don't succeed in the private sector, they will move across to the public sector, which is often more accommodating, and perhaps later move back to the private sector with a whole new set of capabilities and experiences. They are savvy and have worked out ways of making their careers work for them.

The third reason for optimism is the explosion of the internet and observing women set up virtual and online businesses. This is a trend that will only grow.

Also, I am energised by the fact that more women are speaking out and taking a stand. Many of these women are in senior positions and in the past may not have spoken out so vocally. Now they are coming out of the closet and that is a great thing.

Insights for career success

If the CEO is not noisy about the subject in an authentic way, then it may be time to pack your bag of tricks and try elsewhere.

My numerous mentoring discussions over the years with my own staff and with other women have yielded rich data. I find women much more likely than men to 'up stakes' and take risks on their next move or career. The ones with children or who intend to have children are adept at doing 'trade-off' calculations. They actively seek out employers and sectors where they believe they'll better be able to 'have it all'. It is this cohort who so often decides to establish their own business, taking advantage of modern technology to create the sort of flexibility they need.

When they choose employers, their own view — and mine — is that they should head to where there are already women in executive and senior positions. It is those organisations that are most likely to readily accept working mothers' constraints, seek out women for promotion, extend and challenge women and have workplace cultures that women like to be in.

Evidence shows that the strongest predictor of women's progress to senior executive roles is the number of women working in that area. Probable causes are:

- As more women move in and are seen to be successful, there is greater willingness to hire more.

- As women move in, the stereotype of leadership changes and the new, less-male stereotype facilitates the hiring of more women.

Similarly powerful is the opportunity for women to be involved in activities that will advance their careers. This, though, involves managers being good at task delegation — not a common trait.

I advise women to tread warily. Be mindful of the organisation they are targeting: is it one that is good for women, or good for their CV, but not for the soul? The organisations that are good for women are easy to identify — they have more women in senior roles, which makes a huge difference.

Also, look at the CEO because they lay down the culture. Any CEO who is serious about the issue will set targets — not just on numbers of women, but also on implementation of broader initiatives like flexible work practices and part-time work that are accessed by the whole workforce including older workers. Managers must also be held accountable for achieving these targets, including rewards for achievement and sanctions if these targets are not met. After all, all other business priorities will have targets against them. It is difficult to successfully implement part-time work so those organisations who do it well have true commitment. Also, look at the number, style and character of women in senior roles as an indicator of what the CEO values.

Be strategic when questioning the CEO or senior leaders. For instance, find out what are the top, most exciting value-creation opportunities being pursued, how many of their top people are working on them and how many of these are women. Women will wither on the vine if they are not given challenging jobs and challenging projects. A woman can waste a lot of time waiting and thinking some good is going to happen.

Next, undertake research on the company. Read the speeches — what is the HR person giving speeches about? What is the CEO giving speeches about? What is the chief operating officer giving speeches about? The issues the key leaders give airtime to are those they truly value.

The new norm: women are the canary in the mine

In biological terms, lack of diversity is a race to risk and extinction.

Ultimately, CEOs need to hear the following message: if you can't attract, develop and promote women, you know you're losing ground in the labour market and workplace culture. If a bunch of lookalike blokes is the best you can do and the best you want to do, you can be certain you will have a problem. Those blokes are a shrinking pool. The growth is with non-lookalike blokes (Asian men, men who will need to do more parenting than their fathers did or risk losing their relationship) and women.

Paul Waterman
Engaging the Head and the Heart

Paul Waterman was appointed President of BP Australia and New Zealand on 1 September 2010. He is also the Chairman of the Australian Institute of Petroleum and a member of the Business Council of Australia's Growth and Sustainability Committee.

Paul began his career in the oil industry with Castrol North America in 1994. In 2000, BP acquired Castrol and he subsequently held a number of senior positions in fuels retailing in the UK and USA. His role prior to his posting to Australia was Vice President of Castrol Aviation, Industrial, Marine and Energy Lubricants. Before joining BP, he worked in brand management at Kraft Foods and Reckitt Benckiser.

Paul was born in Michigan, USA, and holds a Bachelor of Science from Michigan State University and an MBA in Finance and International Business from the Stern School of Business, New York University.

BP came to my attention through the reputation it has been building for a genuine focus on gender diversity, and I was fascinated to explore how this has come about. I talked to Paul to understand what BP Australia and New Zealand (BP ANZ) have been doing to improve gender diversity, the progress made, and some of the issues and barriers the business is still facing.

When Paul arrived in Australia in 2010, plans were already in place around Diversity & Inclusion, with one of the key elements being a focus on gender diversity, but the business was struggling to gain traction and increase the proportion of female employees, especially in more senior roles. The business had a 31 percent female workforce compared to 69 percent male, and was seeing female resignations running at a higher rate than males. Analysis showed that if women continued to progress into senior roles at the historical rate, the business would achieve gender parity in senior roles in over 100 years' time!

Playing to win

Paul recognises that, for BP ANZ to succeed, it must attract and retain the very best talent. He also understands that, unlike some other places that BP operates in globally, the relative strength of the Australian economy means that talent and key skills are in short supply. His simple premise is that, if you need talent to succeed, it's madness to only seriously access half of the market — the male half. Organisations cannot afford to leave any talent on the table because there simply is not the luxury of having a large pool of qualified people.

Paul believes that if you have an organisation full of people who look similar, have had similar education and work experiences, and have the same social background, you lack the diversity of thinking and ideas to drive innovation and progression.

'When we mix things up, we find that we get an awful lot more innovation.'

BP ANZ has a Diversity, Inclusion & Meritocracy strategy, which follows the premise that to confront an erosion of the talent pipeline and to improve their position, they are best served by being able to attract and retain talent from a more diverse range of people. This has led to a focus on four priority areas in Australia and New Zealand:

1. *Inclusive and meritocratic environment.* To build an inclusive and meritocratic environment where all people can contribute and be successful, ensuring the right people are selected for the right roles.

2. *Gender.* To increase representation and retention of females at all levels.

3. *Indigenous employment.* To increase the proportion of Indigenous employees in the workforce.

4. *Ageing population.* To become an age-friendly workplace.

For BP ANZ, Diversity & Inclusion is about acknowledging, valuing and leveraging similarities and differences for business success. This means creating an environment where all employees are valued and can give their best, opening up access to opportunity for everyone, and ensuring that BP ANZ reflects the local communities in which they work and the true talent pools available to them.

Paul believes passionately that in the context of a shrinking skilled labour pool, to retain talent, bring in new people and obtain discretionary effort, BP ANZ must have a reputation, processes and work climate that not only respects differences, but also leverages them for competitive advantage.

Hearts and minds

BP ANZ has historically spent a lot of time on the left-brain, logical aspects of the diversity argument, and Paul recognises that the focus on the 'head' has been at the expense of engaging the 'heart'. This is something he actually sees as more important.

> *'I don't believe that anyone can put hand on heart and say that it's okay to have a culture where I can thrive because I'm male, and you're structurally disadvantaged because you're female.'*

That's not to say that he doesn't buy the logical argument. He points to the evidence that diverse leadership teams generate a measureable improvement in financial performance (externally 41 percent higher return on equity and 56 percent higher earnings), that higher employee engagement results in higher productivity and profit, and that external stakeholders expect it. But the 'heart' tells him that the work environment we create today will be what our children will experience as they enter the workforce.

Paul sees culture change as the critical challenge for the organisation, but one that is very difficult to bring about given the dependency on the behaviours of 9300 people across two countries and in multiple and often remote locations. What is clear, though, is that he places the concept of meritocracy at the centre of the change.

> *'Meritocracy is everything … this concept means anybody can come in to this company and, no matter what your ethnicity, your sexual orientation, your gender, whatever, you have the same chance to succeed as anybody else, and you'd be able to access the same level of support as anybody else. This is really critical.'*

Paul has introduced culture change of this magnitude before and, while his previous experiences were in the USA, he sees similarities to driving change in the Australia and New Zealand environment.

First, you must get into people's hearts as well as their heads because, fundamentally, the heart is where change starts.

Secondly, recognise that fundamental changes in culture are not going to be done in six months; organisations must keep at it for a long time, and hit it very hard on different levels.

Thirdly, CEOs have to be relentless because there will be a certain segment of the population that says, 'Does he or she really mean it?' If they think you do, they go to the next question, which is, 'Can I outlast him or her?' If you are relentless and pursue the agenda on many different fronts, these people very quickly realise that they won't outlast the CEO because this is actually bigger than the individual CEO — it permeates the whole business at all levels.

Walking the walk

This leads to the obvious question of what BP ANZ have been doing to create this focus that permeates the whole business. As Paul describes, they have actually been doing quite a lot at a number of different levels.

BP ANZ has developed an Australia and New Zealand Diversity, Inclusion & Meritocracy strategy and requires each business unit to develop their own specific plan. The content and progress of each plan is reviewed on a quarterly basis with the respective business heads as part of Paul's Quarterly Performance Review meetings.

BP ANZ recognises and values the role of leadership in creating an environment where people feel respected, valued and are able to contribute their best performance. They have invested heavily in the development of senior and first-level leaders, and by the end of 2013 will have trained over 1000 leaders in a program that focuses on understanding the business case for Diversity & Inclusion, becoming aware of unconscious biases and their impact, and equipping participants with the skills to become more inclusive leaders. In addition, the Virtual Mentoring Program has taken over 70 leaders through a structured, gender-focused program — the men's program helps male participants better understand the case for gender diversity in the workplace and develop skills required to better lead and mentor women, while the women's program upskills females in key areas that are barriers to their career advancement such as gender-based stereotypes, building personal brand, and balancing work and home life. The message is clear and simple: if you want to succeed as a leader at BP ANZ, you must demonstrate that you are committed to, and capable of, building diverse and inclusive teams.

There are clear expectations in place regarding gender diversity in the recruitment of roles. All selection panels must be gender-diverse and have at least one female member. Candidate pools must also be gender-diverse, with the expectation that the shortlist will contain at least one suitably qualified female candidate. Exceptions must be signed off by Paul or the HR director. This has led to line managers thinking more robustly about how to attract female candidates, what the environment needs to look like to attract and retain females, and where to look for suitably qualified female candidates. Paul does point out that meritocracy still applies to the final selection decision.

'This is not about appointing females into roles to meet a target — that's insulting to an individual's capability and bad for the business. It's about creating genuinely diverse and broad talent

pools, but the final decision is always based on merit and appointing the most suitable person for the role.'

The gender focus has been aligned to BP ANZ's key talent initiatives, with the aim of having a minimum 50-percent female intake into the Graduate Program and on internal talent programs such as the Emerging Talent and Career Acceleration programs. In addition, Paul and key members of his leadership team hold 'development conversations' with all females on succession plans for senior-level roles. This has allowed him to get to know individuals, understand their aspirations, and then have a follow-up conversation with their line managers. This process gives the company a much better line of sight on where the talent is located, and what staff are looking for. The response from the staff has been, 'Oh, you want to have a chat with me about my career? That makes me feel good.'

Significant work has also taken place on the environmental elements that are key to attracting and retaining female talent. The gender pay gap has been closed by eight percent over the last three years, and during this period relevant HR policies have been reviewed to ensure greater flexibility, more access to job-sharing arrangements and greater focus on meeting the specific needs of female employees. This has resulted in 91 percent of maternity leavers returning to the organisation in 2012, up from 70 percent in 2009. Additionally, BP ANZ senior leaders have actively sponsored female-focused groups such as BP WIN (BP Women's International Network) and PARTNA (BP ANZ's Part-Time Employee Network).

But one of the most powerful things BP ANZ has been doing is constantly emphasising the importance of gender diversity. Paul talks about it at every opportunity — internally and externally —

and encourages his senior leaders to do the same. Employees see that it is a leadership focus area and is not going away, and is backed up by action through the initiatives being undertaken. It's about leaders 'walking the walk, not just talking the talk'.

All of this effort has resulted in BP being awarded the prestigious Employer of Choice for Women citation, which recognises organisations that have actively improved their external employer brand and attraction of women.

Quota or no quota

Interestingly, BP hasn't gone down the route of hard targets, and the current debate around quotas worries Paul because achieving gender diversity is not a simple question. For Paul, gender diversity is more than just numbers; it is also about having an environment that is inclusive and meritocratic. He agrees that organisations should be held to account for their level of commitment to targets for executives, senior leaders, graduates, emerging leaders, people on the fast track and in the pipeline for future senior roles, but believes that the overall situation is too complex to be a blunt 'all or nothing'. Too much is reliant on the culture of the organisation, and Paul sees that once you change the culture you will never look back; it'll just keep getting better and better. If you only implement a quota and it is not underpinned by culture, systems and process, it simply won't be sustainable.

> *'I think the people calling for quotas are well intentioned; I really believe they want to see change, and they want it to be really fast. But I don't think they are thinking through the unintended consequences of that kind of heavy-handed sort of implementation.'*

Quotas need the leadership team to own them and need to be part of a wider diversity strategy. If quotas for the number of females appointed into senior roles are mandated externally, achieving them for could mean organisations will appoint females to roles they're not ready for and doesn't align with BP's meritocratic approach. Organisations will get the numbers they are required to, but in Paul's view there is a 100-percent certainty that they won't change the culture or create a sustainable pipeline of female talent. In the end they will have simply papered over the cracks. They won't get the head and the heart commitment to diversity. Instead, men will dig in, become cynical and completely back away from the commitment needed. The entire burden will fall on the women and their legitimacy to undertake these roles will be stripped away as they become branded as just a quota woman.

> *'I think every company should be able to prove their level of commitment to making change. But I think where this will go off the rails very quickly [is] if, hypothetically, the government said to me, "You have to have 50 percent of your leadership team female in 18 months. Go, do it."'*

The other danger of quotas is that they tend to focus on senior roles and that only tackles the problem in a small proportion of the organisation. Paul understands the need for a more holistic approach that looks at the issue from multiple angles — something he describes as the push–pull model of intervention.

Push and pull

The challenges of developing gender diversity are significant, but heightened in some of the remote geographical locations where BP ANZ operates where there is even greater competition for talent and is often in short supply. In small terminals, or refineries with workforces that have been in place for 25 or 30 years, effecting the change is more difficult compared to a head office or city environment with a more dynamic workforce. These, and many other factors, inform the unique interventions required at each level: the push–pull model, one that addresses the complexity of gender diversity from several standing points.

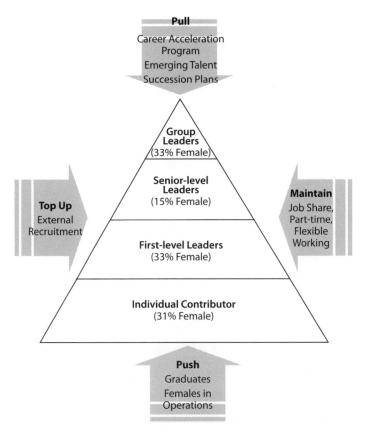

Like any other company, as you move up to the top there are fewer people. The 'pull' programs move people up from first-level leader roles and develop the talent in the business. This is part of the talent management and succession planning for executive and senior-level leaders, ensuring BP has qualified female candidates on its succession plans.

And then there is a 'push' that needs to be made in two key areas. The first is a push in the number of women appointed through the graduate recruitment program. BP ANZ aims for at least 50-percent females and has regularly achieved higher.

> 'The second push is to correct the half-hearted attempts at gender diversity over the last 20 years in which people welcomed women into the organisation and said, "That's great, good that you're here. How about a career in marketing, or human resources, or finance?"'

Females were not pushed towards operational roles, and to be on the trajectory to be CEO of a company requires them to have had 10 or 15 years of operations experience. BP ANZ encourages and facilitates women graduates to transition into some operations roles, and explains how critical that is to their trajectory, explaining that if you're an ambitious woman, you really have to gain some operational experience to understand the different aspects of the business and to be a business leader in the future.

A great example of this was faced by Asset Management, which is BP ANZ's engineering project management division. They had no female employees in operational leadership roles and found that only 16 percent of engineering students are female and that only 10 percent of women with an engineering qualification commence work in the field. This is exacerbated by the fact that of those who start, only 15 percent are still practising their profession by the age of 40. This has started to shift as leadership have become more engaged. The business have reviewed their sourcing strategy, flexible working and maternity leave return options have been actively promoted and the onboarding process has been overhauled.

The Asset Management work is an example of where BP ANZ have tried very hard to retain valuable staff during different stages of their lives — for example, when women commence a family, by implementing a number of programs to keep people connected such as standardising the approach to part-time work. It used to be the case that if your manager was a little more cutting-edge, you'd get approval to work part-time, but other managers often wouldn't let you do that, which creates unfairness in the organisation. So BP ANZ standardised the approach so anybody, male or female, could come forward with a proposal to work part-time. HR will vet it, the person gets a fair hearing, and if their proposal meets the guidelines they get the answer that they're looking for. So it's fair across the entire organisation; it's not dependent on what situation you're in or who your line manager is. As a result, BP ANZ has achieved a post–maternity leave retention rate of 88 percent in 2012, and men are starting to access part-time work in the later years of their working lives.

BP ANZ is also actively promoting job-sharing and has a number of females who are very successfully sharing jobs at professional levels. These women are helping BP ANZ learn about what makes job-share work or not work by putting together guidelines and support information for individuals and line managers considering such an arrangement.

The challenge with increasing the level of flexibility in an organisation is often in doing so at all levels. Paul has challenged BP ANZ to increase the number of job-share arrangements in operational positions 'because you may have small children at home and sometimes it's not easy to be on call 24/7 in an operational role. That's been a barrier, if we have a job-share we can remove that barrier.' The other flexibility challenge he has presented is to be very clear when advertising any job whether or not it can be part-time, a job-share or a full-time role, instead of assuming all roles are full-time, and there needs to be a conversation about anything else.

Job-sharing and working part-time is not necessarily going to be 100-percent successful, but that's okay to Paul — not all new hires (irrespective of gender) have a 100-percent success rate, either. Expecting a perfect result in these flexible work practices all the time is simply not realistic but having them as an option is.

What about the long hours incumbent on many senior roles? Well, it is part of the geographical challenge of working as part of a global organisation in Australia that communication with other parts of the world is often after hours. Nevertheless, this after-hours culture is contained wherever possible. For instance, Paul does not send emails on weekends because he does not want to set up the expectation that managers must respond on a Sunday. The weekend should be their time with family and friends.

The final axis of the push–pull model is the need to 'top up' the female talent pipeline through external recruitment. BP's global downstream business has established processes aimed to create a level playing field for all applicants for roles. All vacancies, including roles filled internally, are required to have a shortlist containing diverse candidates and selection panels that contain diversity. Independent assessment tools are used for many professional roles, and leaders are required to be transparent with the organisation about the process they adopted to select the candidate, including the people involved in the decision.

The never-ending journey

'What we are doing at BP is just a start,' says Paul. 'If we stopped in two years we would have wasted a lot of valuable effort. I know that we still have people who don't get it, so we have to work through that and pull more females up, and push more females into operational roles. 'We can't ever feel like we've made it — it's the same with safety, which is the number-one priority for the BP Group. If you have a week or a month in your business where nobody gets hurt, you can't say, "Well, now we're all safe." The same goes for diversity; you have to keep at it relentlessly.'

Developing your company's culture is a never-ending journey and you have to stay on the path. If you look at companies that don't do well under a variety of different measures, often it's because their culture has not been important to them. So Paul describes striving for a meritocracy as a never-ending labour of love. Everyone must be passionate about how important it is, and give their best towards creating that.

A final measure: BP globally completes employee satisfaction surveys every year, and there are a variety of different questions about culture that they seek. Paul wants high levels of feedback on whether this is a fair place to work, if people feel respected or have access to opportunity, and if they are proud to be a part of the organisation. Diversity is a huge measure of the strength of a culture, so BP monitors that pretty closely, too.

'Word gets around and the more you do, the better people feel. The better people feel, the better the people you attract, and it just kind of keeps going in the right direction.'

Katherine Teh-White

The Secret to Career Happiness

Katherine Teh-White, Founder and Managing Director of Futureye, is no stranger to male-dominated work environments. From journalism to mining and forestry, she has experienced the good, the bad and the ugly of male-dominated corporate cultures. Having travelled a long, hard journey to where she is today, Katherine's touchstone is her personal values. She constantly reflects on these values and her experiences, especially the confronting ones, to continuously learn and grow as an individual and to guide her career journey. She has also made some unique discoveries about how women can achieve happiness through a 'state of flow', creating alignment between their individual selves, the organisation and society.

Lessons for planning your career success:
The 'Magnificent Seven'

Katherine's current role as Managing Director of Futureye, a consulting firm that helps businesses identify and manage public concerns about their operations, is the culmination of a long journey of reflection and learning and a natural extension of her personal values, passions and drivers. Here is her journey and seven key magnificent lessons she has drawn out of life's experiences.

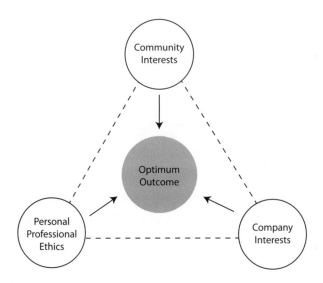

1. The mother of all lessons: the path to happiness is alignment between the individual, the organisation and society.

The triangulation of these three components — your individual self, your organisation and your place in society — helps you understand your place in the world and provides you with a sense of meaning and purpose. If you can work in an organisation that fulfils your individual desires, uses your personal and professional skills, stretches your professional capacity, and delivers societal outcomes that you think are important, you will always be in flow.

Katherine drew on the work of Mihaly Csikszentmihalyi, known as the architect of the concept of *flow*, which arose from his study of happiness and creativity.[1] Being in flow is like being 'in the zone' or 'in the groove': you are fully immersed, engaged and fulfilled by what you are doing. Reaching a state of flow, according to Csikszentmihalyi, means moving up various stages of development by becoming expert at one level, then, when that level is conquered, moving on to the next, higher level. This could explain why computer games are so addictive, particularly those that move you step by step to higher levels of achievement.

Katherine experiences flow in her work because she has developed her triangle — there is a strong alignment between what she does in her working and non-working life, utilisation of the skills she has built up over the years, and the social objectives of the organisation she works with. Fulfilment is derived from the interplay between her values, her aspirations for a better society, and how she works to achieve that society and runs her life.

How has this concept shaped her career transition decisions? Well, Katherine has always had a keen sense of what she believed was important and how she wanted to help shape society. At 15 years of age, she had already written her public policy platform for Australia!

If you want to change the world, says Katherine, you need to know how it works. So she became a journalist to learn 'how the world works'. Her next career move, into a large mining conglomerate some six years later, was a deliberate move away from 'watching and reporting on the world' towards participation and being able to have an impact on it. Her position was as Community Issues Adviser, and her task was to anticipate and resolve problems that may prevent major project approvals from being granted.

This became extraordinarily challenging for a 23-year-old in a industrial culture more interested in 'wrestling crocodiles' other than community ones. She resigned and went to work for Western Mining, whose CEO, Hugh Morgan, understood the need for change in regard to community relations and wanted to see that change happen. This vision was far more aligned with her own.

Futureye was established by Katherine in 2002, a business born from her realisation that every reputational crisis she had seen in large corporations had come about because of a mismatch at the individual, organisation and societal levels. Establishing her own business enabled her to contribute to her vision of sustainable development for the world.

2. *Know yourself*

Katherine drew inspiration from the famous French artist Henri Matisse. Looking through the history of his artwork, one can see that Matisse had an incredible eye for detail. He understood his craft in a very detailed way, and this became the foundation for being able to simplify his art over time yet also break new ground in art. Similarly, in a work context, Katherine believes, understanding the details of your skill set and having deep insight into your capabilities can provide you with a realistic appreciation of what can be achieved. Successful leaders constantly evaluate their skill set and strive for deep insight into their capabilities. They don't just draw on past experience but attempt to visualise what the future looks like and gain clarity about how to get there.

Successful leaders also reflect on their feelings, understand the factors that lead them to feeling outraged about something, and can communicate their feelings sufficiently early in a situation, without getting overexcited. The lack of an outlet to express feelings of outrage is a risk management factor that many organisations seem to overlook. Self-reflection and expression of feelings are important emotional regulation strategies and can move you beyond feelings of bitterness about negative experiences into a state of empowerment.

Katherine has experienced being outraged at work. In one job, a powerful male executive threatened to ruin her career if she did not meet his sexual demands. The perpetrator remained in the organisation and Katherine felt there was no option other than to resign. Anecdotally, we know that this is a common organisational response. Katherine had naïvely believed that you can achieve success simply through hard work, focus and doing a good job. That rule worked for her until this incident, at age 28. Reality hit her that the decision on who to back was not based on any business case for value contributed, but on power — who he knows, who he has backed in the past. She felt a strong sense of outrage and couldn't believe that all her contributions to the business had come to nothing. Possibly if there was a view that the organisation would benefit from taking a 'victim-centric' approach to understanding the issues, things may have been different.

3. Don't be afraid of failures:
They are your greatest learing opportunities

Every single failure enables you to develop and grow new skills. Looking back on this time, Katherine realises that it was one of her greatest learning experiences. What did she learn? Well, one lesson was that meritocracy — being good at your job — is not enough. The network within an organisation matters. So, yes, you need to be good at your job, but you also need to pay attention to the social network around you at work.

Related to failure is having an understanding of your weaknesses. One of Katherine's most humorous moments came when she was interviewed for a cadetship at *The Age* newspaper. This was a hugely competitive process. Around 2000 people sat the exam, and only around 100 passed to the interview stage. At the interview she was asked, 'So, Katherine, what is your greatest weakness?' and she replied, 'Writing.' The interviewer laughed and said, 'Well, why would you want to be a journalist then?' She responded, 'Because I want to get better at it.'

4. Understand the rules of the game

The rules of the game are the unspoken rules, sometimes the insidious ways in which people operate in an organisation. They determine who will succeed and how. As a newspaper cadet, Katherine learned that one of the rules of the game was that it didn't matter what level you worked in at the paper; if you were able to secure an exclusive story, it would be yours. One of her favourite filmmakers of all time is Woody Allen. Allen's new movie was coming out so she rang the Australian representative of the movie company and was told there wouldn't be an interview with Allen made available in Australia. She really wanted to do this interview so she stayed up late, found out who the New York agent for Allen was, wrote to them, phoned them and generally badgered them as much as she dared until she had convinced them to give *The Age* newspaper and herself an interview. So, as a 19-year-old cadet, she had secured an interview with the world-famous Woody Allen.

She went to the Chief of Staff and said, 'I got an interview. I got an exclusive interview with Woody Allen!' Her boss was concerned about Katherine's lack of seniority, but as she said, 'They're the rules.' So she stuck by them. Then, of course, Katherine had to worry about how she could deliver it!

On another game-playing level, women in male-dominated working environments also need to be mindful of the rules. This can be a controversial view among some women, yet women do need to desensitise themselves and develop a resilient attitude in some workplaces — not to the point of being harassed or bullied, but by not overreacting to situations. The key is getting the balance right: you don't want to be so desensitised that you don't feel the impacts of workplace violence issues. On the other hand, you don't want to be so reactive that people conclude you can't manage the identification and resolution of issues effectively in the workplace. We do not generally have gender-neutral workplaces. Women entering into male-dominated work environments need to understand the different paradigms and ways to succeed. In other words, understand the rules of the game — both the rules about how to be successful and how you fail.

5. Back yourself and challenge the norms

Katherine recalled presenting to a group of industrial relations managers about why she thought their industrial relations plan wouldn't work. She put forward what she thought should be the industrial relations plan, which would increase productivity, reduce workers' compensation and achieve a greater level of support for the project.

All the men in the room laughed at her and called her naïve. At that point, she'd never been more furious but she didn't have an industrial relations degree to prove her position, just the intuition. Not one to let an issue she was passionate about lie, she discussed it with her boss, who discussed it with his boss and they approved her strategy, which worked. It did reduce workers' compensation. It did increase productivity.

Her lesson from this experience was that challenging the normal way things had been done and offering alternative ways is important; however, an organisation cannot keep individually challenging norms — it is too risky. Ultimately, it needs to systemise successful approaches and embed them in a culture. Challenging the status quo is not enough — it needs to be accompanied by a plan that enables a concept to become a systematic approach.

6. *Let continuous learning be your guide*

Katherine strongly believes in consciously identifying and targetting organisations that have a learning environment. All organisations say they are or aspire to be a learning organisation, but how can you identify the ones that truly live it? The answer, says Katherine, is to probe how they handle employees' concerns and issues. Ask yourself or your peers some of the following questions about your working environment:

- What are some of the issues that you see inside the organisation?
- How comfortable do people feel about raising these issues and concerns?
- Are there issues that people are too afraid to raise?
- How confident are they that these issues or concerns will be resolved?
- How do leaders deal with being challenged?
- How do they recognise and manage group-think?
- To what extent do they encourage provocative thinking?
- How future-oriented are they?

These are also great due diligence questions you can ask prospective employers.

7. Can't do it on your own

Katherine has gathered a large number of mentors around her at various stages of her career and actively cultivated mentors in people whom she respects and from whom she can learn. Her mentors range from associates she has worked with to a chair of a multinational corporation. She has learned an enormous amount from her mentors: from governance and operational management of her business, through to understanding the minds of a CEO or board chair — in fact, even how men at that level talk to each other. She is convinced she could never have taken her business to its current level without the support of her chosen mentors.

Life as an outsider

From where did these life lessons stem? Not surprisingly, her early childhood had a great impact on Katherine. Her father is Chinese Malaysian and her mother is a fifth-generation Australian. Katherine herself was born in Australia but the family moved to Malaysia for six years soon after. As a six-year-old migrating back to Australia with her family, she considered herself Australian, yet spoke only Chinese and did not look like all the other mainly white, Anglo-Saxon children at her school. One of her teachers at school laughed at her when she identified as an Australian. She experienced the world as an outsider would. She also had a sister who was deaf and observed how she struggled in a community that put up barriers to her being able to be her best and did not accommodate difference. Her mother led the way in changing the educational opportunities for deaf children, believing the current situation for her deaf daughter was unfair and had to change. These early experiences profoundly influenced Katherine's value set and helped refine her thinking around the role of the individual and society.

Life as an outsider taught her how to manage conflict from a very young age, which translated in adult life to having a level of intuition about how others feel, that she may not have otherwise developed. These experiences, believes Katherine, has enabled her to step in and around different stakeholder perspectives and engage with people in ways that matter to them.

Is being an outsider important in developing a kind of intuition about people and what is happening around you? It's not everything, but many people who are very talented in conflict-resolution often have had an experience of feeling like an outsider or being other than the norm and have learned how to manage and deal with conflict.

In summary, here are some of Katherine's insights about how women can futureproof their careers:

- Be clear about what you stand for, your passions and what matters to you as a person. List all the things that have ever made you angry, that enraged you, or made you excited.

- Then, be true to yourself and your passions. Stand up for what you believe. Challenge peer-group thinking.

- Constantly evaluate the reality of your skill set and your capabilities to ensure that your view of what you can achieve is realistic and you can continually develop level by level.

- Know the rules of the game and work out how you can achieve something for the organisation and build something for yourself at the same time.

- Personal reflection and communication are the keys to being emotionally intelligent. Talk it out or risk becoming bitter and negative.

- Be good at your job and just as good at developing a social network within a corporation and industry.

- Do your due diligence. Find a learning organisation where you will be able to realise your potential, level by level.

- Don't try to do it on your own. Mentors can be hugely influential.

- When the fit is no longer there, leave.

Kathleen Townsend
What the Headhunters Don't Tell You

 Kathleen Towsend, Managing Director of Kathleen Townsend Executive Solutions, has been in the executive search and selection sector for 16 years — initially as a Partner at Amrop International, one of the four largest global search firms, before establishing her own firm in 1999. Kathy's earlier career was in public policy and social policy, including with the Office of the Status of Women, for which she was appointed Head in 1994. Her firm has developed a reputation for providing a broad base of CEO and senior executive candidates to organisations across all sectors. She is also known for encouraging organisations to think outside the square regarding potential candidates and to broaden the talent pool by including senior executive women. Around 40 percent of appointments made to CEO and GM roles through Kathleen Townsend Executive Solutions are women.

Leading practices and lagging mindsets

Reflecting on trends in organisations over the last 17 years, Kathy has seen some significant changes. In her view, many contemporary leaders have a much more responsible approach to the world of work when it comes to people practices and behaviours, but she also observes that some old attitudes prevail in the minds of the same leaders, which are in conflict with these new approaches. There have also been changes among the women themselves.

One change Kathy has observed has been the seismic shift in the number of women applying for, or being promoted to, the top ranks. Many more women are prepared to have a go at senior roles, and they increasingly expect that they will achieve them. Still, the numbers are nowhere close to parity with men.

At the same time, many women have made a very clear decision to reject the competitive corporate environment and are leaving in droves to set up their own very successful businesses. Some of the women interviewed for this book are good examples. This is often a conscious decision made by women, who say, 'I don't like the culture of the organisations I have experienced and I'm going to do it a different way.' Kathy believes women are often more objective about their job satisfaction than men, and would probably make the bold decisions to leave earlier in their career than many men.

Another change is the inexorable shift towards flexible working arrangements to accommodate children and family responsibilities. These flexibilities will become more diverse as people start to engage with work in an even more variable way by working from home or from 'hubs'. Some of this is driven by the efforts of companies to be an employer of choice and to recognise and attract a wider talent pool.

Men as well as women are increasingly taking up these flexible arrangements, including taking time out to become a competitive sportsperson, or take up part-time studies, or fulfil childcare responsibilities. However, many decision-makers are still slow to recognise the value of these more flexible working arrangements. Much of the corporate world still believes that if you work part-time you are not serious about your career and that working long hours is the only way to demonstrate commitment.

Yet the business case for working fewer hours or even part-time is compelling. For one thing, these employees are highly productive. Women, having taken advantage of flexible working arrangements for longer, have proven themselves to be very efficient. They are very good at managing their time and getting work done in order to get out of the office by, say, 5pm to meet their 6pm childcare pick-up responsibilities. They don't stand around the water cooler, chatting, or come in early just to be seen. Additionally, employers who are more engaged in the outside world can bring a broader perspective to work, which is often more attractive to a corporation. In contrast, people who work excessive hours a week, for work is all they live and breathe, are at risk of burning out and are unable to bring a wider perspective to their job. They don't shop, or talk to people in their local community, or engage much with their family and wider circles. Their narrow worldview often restricts their ability to think broadly about strategic issues.

'I was talking to an Operations Director who starts work at 6am when the factory starts, while the other managers generally start at 8 or 8.30am. His wife is a barrister and they share the arrangement to pick up the kids and cook the family dinner. He does this twice a week. When he leaves at 3pm, the

rest of the management team question what he is doing. He has been at work since 6am anyway, and will log on to work later at night, but there is an expectation by his colleagues that he's not really doing a full day's work because he's not doing it when they are. If they looked at what his outputs were rather than what the input was, they would have a different view of it.'

What the headhunters look for (that they may not tell you)

As a rule, Kathy does not specifically give advice to women that she would not give to men. So the following list of attributes could apply equally to any candidate. On the other hand, women do have some unique advantages and perspectives, which we will outline a little later.

Here are Kathy's nine pieces of advice that will ensure you pass the headhunter's steely gaze and critical assessment:

1. *Be highly self-aware.* This is the number-one trait that Kathy looks for in men and women she considers for general manager or CEO roles. Self-awareness is knowing your strengths and weaknesses, understanding how you work and how you come across to people, articulating your strengths, and understanding your preferred way of behaving and how that impacts on other people.

2. *Demonstrate a strong track record.* Self-awareness is essential but not sufficient — you must also have a track record of having done the hard yards. This is about staying the course in a role and an organisation for long enough to be able to experience the outcomes of your decisions. Doing the time in roles is important, as it demonstrates that there is substance to your work and that you have worked through the difficult times, not just the exciting times of change. As a rough rule

of thumb, you need three to five years of tenure in a role to demonstrate great achievements or positive outcomes. Executives who move every few years may be well networked, but a headhunter may conclude there is little substance to their work, as they have not stayed around to deliver in the longer term. They may not have learned from their successes and, just as importantly, from their failures.

3. *Don't oversell.* Employers are not going to respond well to an approach that says: 'Here is a list of all my achievements and why I am a fantastic person.' This approach can come across as very self-centred and lacks focus as to what the company wants. A more successful approach is to undertake thorough research to understand the key issues facing the employer. Then, turn the conversation around to put yourself in their shoes so that you are discussing their needs and what they want. The approach could sound something like: 'I understand this is what you're trying to do, and I think I can help you because I bring this track record and set of capabilities.' In this way, you are solving their problems rather than sounding brash and singing you own tune.

4. *Demonstrate breadth.* As a general rule, if you are a CEO candidate, position yourself as a generalist who can lead people, not as a content specialist. As a senior leader or CEO, you need to understand what the business is about, manage budgets and make the tough decisions. You need to attract, inspire and retain the best people for the business. This is where women sometimes are seen as having the advantage — they are often perceived as being excellent at motivating and leading people, having a more collaborative style and a better ability to deal with conflict.

5. *Have self-confidence.* Successful candidates are, among other things, confident and comfortable in their own skin — and don't look too eager. Overeagerness can be interpreted as desperation. Part of this persona of confidence relates to your personal presentation. A simple, and common, error made by women is buying a new suit for an interview because you think you will look good in it, then you sit down and it gapes at the front and you are terribly self-conscious the whole way through. Kathy has also seen women who put on false nails for an interview and tap their nails on the table the whole way through (yes, really!). Although minor, these things can be totally distracting for the interviewer, and they destroy your composure, look unprofessional and detract from the message you want to convey.

6. *Do a great job in your current role.* Your reputation and what others are saying about you is what will land you the job, not what you say about yourself. Be aware that, like it or not, corporates will undertake their own reference-checking using their own networks, over and above the formal reference-checking completed by a search consultant.

7. *Show your vulnerabilities.* Be prepared to talk about your true weaknesses and how you manage them, along with your failures and the lessons you learned from them. Candidates who claim they have never had failures are either being naïve, misleading the interviewer, or running the risk of the prospective employer concluding they are about to experience their first failure at the employer's expense.

8. *Be honest about reasons for leaving employers.* It is a legitimate reason to say, for instance, that you did not get on with your boss, or that the job did not turn out to be what you thought it would. The reason is only a problem if it becomes a pattern.

9. *Listen to the search consultants.* Don't apply for roles if they advise you that you are not suited. It is very difficult for an individual to appreciate the competition he or she is up against when applying for a role. If you are not right for the job and the search consultant tells you that your profile is not what they are looking for, do not waste your time or theirs by insisting on applying anyway. Apart from demonstrating poor judgment and poor self-awareness on your part, your self-esteem will get battered by a rejection that you could have avoided.

Specific advice just for women

There are some unique circumstances women face in managing their careers that require special attention. Here are four additional pieces of advice:

1. *Competing against men with extensive operational experience.* Women can be seen to be at a disadvantage in traditionally male-dominated organisations, often because they lack the hard operational or field experience. Although opportunities in these sectors seem to be stacked against women candidates, women possess some unique strengths that they should highlight. Kathy points out, for instance, that women are more than capable of taking a generic set of skills and personal attributes essential to being a successful general manager or chief executive, and applying them in a whole range of different positions, organisations and sectors. Rather than trying to compete against men with extensive field or operational experience, women could position this lack of experience as an advantage and play to their strengths. For example, if you haven't come up through the traditional operational ranks, you can provide a different perspective that breaks out of

the conventional mindset employers often possess. This new approach can be refreshing especially for an organisation that needs a new direction.

'I can remember talking to one of the four banks about marketing and saying, "Which bank is better at marketing than you are?" And the answer was, "None of them." So, I asked, "Then why would we go and get a marketer from another bank? Wouldn't you want to get someone from a totally different background?"'

This sounds okay in theory, but does it work in practice? Kathy recalls working with an insurance client with a disastrous track record of CEOs, to the point where the management team was imploding. The board decided they needed someone completely different. They told her: 'We don't want anybody that anyone here knows. We need someone who can come in and start all over again and rebuild this, because it's a total mess.' They weren't necessarily looking for a woman, but they were open to somebody who had a very different approach and who did not represent anything that they'd already had. So Kathy's firm brought in a woman from the health sector. She was a brilliant CEO with great general management skills, a sound track record of working through difficult experiences in Australia and the UK, really good at crisis management, and had a strong budget focus. She did a great job. She ran the company for five or six years and totally turned the business around, yet she was new to when she started. Sure, a man could have turned the company around, too, but in Kathy's experience, women are often more open to making the bold move across sectors.

2. *Flexible hours — if, how and when to raise the issue.* Women
    often ask Kathy about when to raise the issue of flexible hours
    or part-time work during a selection process. Her advice is
    not to use part-time work as a bargaining chip when applying
    for a full-time role. Be clear upfront if that is a requirement,
    especially when the role is advertised as a full-time role. The
    other time to ask for flexible or shorter hours is once you are
    employed in an organisation and people trust you, understand
    what you do, and you have established a reputation for being
    reliable, loyal and delivering against expectations.

3. *Finding the right organisational fit.* If you are looking for
    an organisation that truly values women and has selection
    processes based on merit, look at the numbers of women
    in executive positions in these organisations. Ask about the
    affirmative action practices in place that allow people to be
    considered on their merit. For instance, as far back as Kathy's
    time, heading the Inquiry into the Status of Women in Federal
    Government in 1992, government departments had in place
    diverse interview panels, processes to encourage women to
    apply for roles, and an increasing number of senior women
    in the Senior Executive Service. There was an expectation in
    this environment that women would apply, that they would
    be deemed acceptable and that there would be no barriers to
    their appointments. These departments have a mindset that
    doesn't differentiate between women and men. On the other
    hand, organisations that don't reflect on or adopt these types
    of processes tend to rely on their informal networks, which
    can preclude people they don't already know and who don't fit
    into that pre-existing norm of what they think is acceptable. In
    many cases, those people are women.

4. *Selling yourself and your achievements.* Kathy has observed
    that women more often than men tend to undersell
    themselves and often talk about what they can't do. Men are
    often more comfortable talking about their achievements
    rather than what they have not done. Unfortunately, there
    are still examples of double standards in the way men
    and women are assessed for a role. Women often walk a
    fine line in asserting their capabilities but not appearing
    overly ambitious in the minds of the interviewers, whereas
    interviewers seem to be more comfortable with men talking
    about their achievements as a normal expectation. This may
    create unconscious bias in the selection process — something
    that interviewers need to be aware of. The search consultant
    is there to raise the self-confidence of candidates and ensure
    they perform at their best at the client interview. Ask for their
    advice about the style most suited to the client and practice
    with the consultant if you have the opportunity.

Conclusion

In a nutshell, the profile of a successful candidates is someone
who possesses a comprehensive resume with the right background
(which could be a varied background) and a substantial track
record that demonstrates they have done the groundwork. They
are very thorough and well-prepared. They have thought through
what the role involves and how they might approach it. They have
a sense of direction about where both the role and the broader
organisation might go, and they provide the client with a sense
of confidence that they can guide the organisation and its staff to
that point.

How do you stack up?

Hugh Davies

Drawing Some Conclusions about
Career Management in the Current Decade

Hugh Davies's career has traversed the gamut of human resources roles. Beginning with Rio Tinto and working in Broken Hill and North Wales, industrial relations and recruitment were his responsibility. He returned to Australia and joined Mobil in Brisbane, where he held a generalist role, followed by a compensation and benefits focus in Melbourne. He then moved to Singapore to oversee human resources management for Mobil in Singapore, Malaysia and Thailand. Back in Australia, Hugh joined Mayne Nickless as Head of Human Resources for 14 years. Subsequently, he made a sideways move into the career transition services sector, working with Right Management Consultants for seven years before establishing Macfarlan Lane, a specialist career transition firm focusing on senior-level assignments, in 2004.

Some fundamental truths

The examples of great career building in this book all demonstrate some fundamental truths about how success can be achieved:

- Most successful individuals take charge of their own careers: they adopt a direction for perhaps just a five- or six-year period, using this time to capture experience and opportunities. These become the foundation for their next career move. They don't rely on others to build their careers for them — and they don't plan in particular detail beyond just a few years ahead — because too much can change in organisations, technology and personal circumstances in a full working lifetime.

- Most of us are influenced by the examples of others whom we admire. We learn and develop professionally by emulating the behaviours, values and practices of successful people around us. Likewise, successful individuals almost always find good mentors, people whose advice they respect.

- Successful individuals also build career resilience: the ability to set directions, navigate changes in circumstances, and overcome setbacks and poor leadership in others, and above all remain comfortable in their own skin. They are not hostage to the opinions of others.

It seems that successful people — those who live full and authentic lives — combine a mix of humility and willingness to learn, with a comfortable sense of self: a steady inner compass, a set of values and practices and self-control. It is interesting to reflect on where this inner confidence comes from. How much of this quality is a function of temperament, how much is it the gift of good parenting, and how much is welded together through the intelligence and flexibility of the individual and their observations of others?

The nature of career development

The 'career' part of our lives can be as challenging as our childhood and adolescent years, our maturing as young adults, and our learning to sustain relationships, be a parent and grow old. In our career lives we are also challenged, and we learn, experiment, observe and experience continuously. Opportunities can be handed to us, changes can come unexpectedly, and career progress can rest on personal strengths and character as much as on experience. In short, navigating a career can be stressful.

Sometimes, in the context of our career strategy work at Macfarlan Lane, we get to work with very bright individuals who have shoehorned themselves into the 'wrong' career: one that does not match their interests or natural capabilities. Individuals in the wrong careers may be capable enough to have 'handled' their chosen careers adequately, but the cost to their personal lives and inner stress can be considerable. Enduring success in senior roles, with work–life balance and satisfaction, seems to rest on clear self-insight into what one is good at and enjoys, and what might best be avoided.

People taking up progressively more senior roles can also sometimes become seriously invested in their work. It seems some roles and some careers require this. The journey to partnership in a law firm, for example, or in a professional firm can be very demanding, requiring knowledge and skills acquisition, building client relationships and holding together a substantial practice area for the firm. The journey and accession to a CEO role is a very demanding process with huge pressures on time, energy and focus.

The rewards might be terrific, in status and in financial terms, but so too is the demand. Many senior individuals, understandably, end up defining themselves largely by their careers. It seems they are first a CEO, or a partner, and then secondly a family man or woman with another set of relationships and living to complete. These 'lives' can be conflicting and often give rise to pressures and costs. There are exceptional individuals who can remain balanced — but, for most, the stresses involved in building career success limit the oxygen given to the other lives they might otherwise enjoy.

For the most part, the stories in the book are the stories of women who have avoided these costs and consequences. Quite possibly, the challenges of being women in an imperfect organisational world have helped them avoid this outcome.

In an ideal world, careers should give value to the whole business of personal growth and fulfilment. There is a lot to be said for periodically taking a step back to examine the balance of our lives. Few of us get all of the efforts and rewards right, all of the time. It would be nice to think, though, that success might be seen in broader terms than just that of the career.

One small risk in asking individuals to look back on their careers is that sometimes the stories make their careers look much better planned and sequential than they in fact were. As we have seen, careers and career changes can be messy, sometimes unanticipated and rough. One abiding truth, looking at each story in this book, is how inner strength and resilience counts for so much in navigating the rough bits. There is also a lot to be said for a bit of disruption: for taking time out to really reflect on what matters in the business of designing a good life. It may not be your choice to be 'out of a job' for a time, but many good people use this time to take stock and to design new, better directions.

Developing some useful perspectives

This is a book of stories about interesting, successful leaders. It was decided that they should all be women, quite deliberately. And they have been asked, again quite deliberately, to take that step back to examine their careers and explain to us what they have done and how they did it. In her introduction, Norah Breekveldt asks, 'Why this book and why now?' The answer to 'Why now?' is because the increasing contribution of women in the workforce over the last few decades is not matched by a relative increase in representation in the upper echelons of the business and professional worlds. There is a great deal of research attempting to understand and explain this, yet very little has changed.

So the answer to 'Why this book?' is that anecdotal evidence — the stories in this book — show that change can happen and also how it can happen. The women in this book are exemplars for other hardworking, ambitious and dedicated women attempting to 'break the glass ceiling', or have an impact on something they are passionate about, or build a sustainable business.

Although there is rarely a glass ceiling for men, these women's stories are relevant to men as well because they illustrate many of the principles that support successful career transitions of the kind that many senior males also strive for. These are: being prepared to move sideways; avoiding traps or situations that may bog you down; flexibility and a preparedness to move on; an ability to seize opportunities and ignore barriers; the need to build on or drawn from a supportive family or network; recognising strengths and weaknesses; perseverance; passion; drive, energy and enthusiasm.

Another conclusion from these stories is that most of our protagonists seem to take a self-employed perspective even when developing their careers in the envelopes of corporations and larger organisations. Just as start-up businesses need clear skills and competencies, so too do those aiming for CEO and leadership roles.

For all of us, I think, it is really worth looking to see how these competencies are expressed and demonstrated in others we respect — and then working out how to create working practices of our own that will deliver the same talents and achievements. The successful women leaders profiled in this book are exemplars of great career management: people who have taken charge of their own careers and made their way through the many hurdles aspiring women face. I think their stories illustrate wider truths in career management, many of them applicable to both genders.

Fresh career thinking: insights developed in Macfarlan Lane

Norah and I both work in a career strategy business that specialises in working with senior individuals, and the people we have worked with have helped us build some reasonably good insights into careers development and career transition.

There are three useful perspectives in navigating careers. The first is that great careers are built on a pretty good understanding of yourself: your signature strengths and what you want and value. The second perspective is that careers — all careers — need a 'market': people or organisations who need what you plan to deliver, where the opportunity to do this is feasible, and where the price (salary or fee) is fair. And, thirdly, there are a bunch of tools and skills needed (including resumes, interview skills, intelligence-gathering skills), which help immensely in capturing opportunities.

I should explain these in a little more detail.

There are many tools and instruments to help individuals map out core capabilities, strengths, skills, preferences and values. Some are simple, and some involve personality profiling and psychological assessments. At Macfarlan Lane we use several in our career transition practice, but with senior people one of the most effective is simply to ask individuals to talk about and write up their key achievements. The essence is one of identifying the opportunity or challenge, what the individual did (getting to the 'how' and the context), and then a summary of the outcome. From this work, it is but a short step to work up strong conclusions about capabilities. (There is a great deal else we derive from this work, by the way.)

Capabilities important in senior roles are a mix of built skills (for example, strategy formation, business analysis and particular fields of knowledge) and underlying competencies (such as communication and influencing skills, leadership and emotional intelligence).

Senior people who have been operating effectively in demanding roles for some time usually draw on both built skills and strong inherent capabilities. But most will have also carefully chosen roles that do not require talents they lack — or they have carefully built up support where this is needed. These people are far more likely to be happy and content with their career paths.

Moving on to the second useful perspective or platform, great careers are also built on an astute sense of a good 'market' — an opportunity where your particular mix of capabilities and interests will be valued. These may exist within organisations, or beyond them, and may become open when people move on or when new activities open up. Unfortunately, some individuals condemn themselves to periods of great frustration, aiming for opportunities where there are fairly thin prospects.

Some senior people we have spoken with about moving on from senior roles, for example, believe they will 'pick up a few directorships' and work part-time in a portfolio of such roles. Some CEOs we work with assume their strong track record means they will take only a short time to be offered another CEO role. The fact is that roles in both markets are scarce. The issue to be dealt with is not about how good or capable an individual is; it is more about a limited supply of openings, and a reasonably large number of contenders. A multifaceted approach becomes needed, with interim activity sometimes involved, in reaching a desired outcome.

The individuals we work with explore markets through the obvious channels: conversations with search consultants and by reviewing what is said in advertisements, the press, organisation websites, analysts reports and business databases. The most effective channel in building both knowledge and visibility is through business intelligence interviewing. This is our term for networking discussions based on thoughtful questions.

'Markets' for employment can also be created by considering self-employment — a pathway implemented by some of those whose stories make up this book. The line between regular employment in a corporate body or in government, and founding a brand-new entrepreneurial venture, is long and fuzzy. Along it will be found partners in law and professional services firms, professionals starting new practices, interim (or contract) executives, people buying into businesses, consultants, business start-ups, project managers and IT gurus, people winning directorships, joining non-profits, mentoring, teaching, starting bed-and-breakfasts, and buying franchises. This continuum covers full- and part-time work, and irregular as well as regular employment.

The success of a career, or career transition, can be enhanced if a wide canvas including forms of self-employment is considered. The self-employment pathway may only be actually launched by a few who have a clear skill set for self-employment (and who have identified a strong market for their services), but it does open up useful thinking and a possible 'next career' after the last job. Ironically, a little time invested here alongside regular job-search activity tends to make the people we work with more attractive to larger firms.

It is interesting to see how some of the subjects of this book took this adventure. Increasingly, self-employment is becoming a part, or one of, the several careers successful people build for themselves.

The third element needed in navigating careers (and career changes, in particular) is something of a toolkit of skills and resources. No rocket science here. Individuals needing to land new opportunities have to learn how to research markets, how to gather direct intelligence (networking), how to deal with recruiters and search firms (and, increasingly, social networking channels such as LinkedIn), how to interview effectively and how, finally, to negotiate a good outcome. There are good books and, of course, many people offering advice in these areas. At senior levels the advice needs to come from peer level consultants and be accompanied by rich resources in relation to research and other services.

This leads me back to some final comments on the inner qualities associated with successful career building and career resilience — because resilience is something all of the women in this book have demonstrated in spades.

Developing career resilience really means developing durable and independent competencies that enable us to fashion and guide our own careers as well as our personal lives.[1] Some years ago, I came to the view that the ideal set of competencies to work on here are predominantly those of emotional intelligence with a bit of IQ thrown in. I thought the best kitbag of values and practices that underpin these career building capabilities would include:

- *Self-control and self-management.* Belief in yourself and an ability to not be dragged down by self-criticism. Taking charge of your own development and training, learning by doing, being unafraid of making mistakes. A disciplined focus on learning and on the development of solutions to difficulties.

- *Initiative/proactivity.* Self-direction and an ability to take risks. Looking to prompt and lead change rather than waiting on the actions of others. An inner sense of direction.

- *Empathy.* Accepting and seeking to understand the feelings and emotions of others rather than being quick to make judgments.

- *Effectiveness with others.* Appreciation of group processes and the identity individuals gain in groups. Ability to lead by giving others ownership of decisions and actions. Achieving effective influence with others by being a good listener.

- *Analytic thinking.* Being acquisitive for knowledge, with a readiness to collect and analyse data, thinking through its implications.

The successful subjects of each of the stories in this book illustrate — or demonstrate — very strongly the competencies summarised here.

Ultimately, those kind enough to give Norah their time for this book made their own way, often moving sideways to success. They worked with well-developed self-insight and courage in tackling hurdles and prejudice and indifference. Most sought out good advice from time to time, and moved to new opportunities or markets as the need arose, without looking back. All built a measure of resilience. At a personal level, I think this is a blend of self-control, proactivity, an understanding of other people, relationship-building skills, some leadership, and of course a cool head and hard analysis from time to time. This wonderful set of competencies was no doubt tested often in the sometimes messy, unpredictable world of work.

A Checklist for Successful Career Navigation

Gathering intelligence and conducting some simple research around your possible career choices is important from three different perspectives:

1. From personal reflection on your own offer to the market, anchored in signature strengths, passions and interests.

2. From the perspective of target organisations, what they stand for and how they may meet your needs.

3. Around the CEO or leader you may be working with and their ability to help you realise your potential.

Each of these perspectives is further outlined below.

The person

- Insight into your values, what you stand for and your passions

- Clear understanding of signature strengths, capabilities and interests

- Clarity around what you want to do

- Ability to articulate achievements, capabilities and contribution

- What 'balance' and 'fulfilment' mean in the context of your career

A Checklist for Successful Career Navigation

Personal checklist

- Be clear about what you stand for, your mission in life, your passions and what matters to you as a person. List all the things that excite you or enrage you.

- Be true to yourself and your passions. Stand up for what you believe in. Challenge peer-group thinking.

- Constantly evaluate the reality of your skill set and your capabilities to ensure that your view of what you can achieve is realistic and you can continually develop, level by level.

- Be clear about what is important to you at work — those elements that are essential to you, and those you must avoid.

- Be good at your job, seek out challenging work and document your achievements.

- Be good at developing a social network within a corporation.

- Understand when the time comes to leave. When the fit between your capabilities and potential and the needs of the organisation is no longer there, it may be time to move on.

The organisation

- Market intelligence — reputation among women

- Has a track record in diversity

- Where women are positioned — role and seniority

- Style of women in the organisation

- What leaders pay attention to in both talk and action

- A learning culture that demonstrates it values diversity of thinking

- Understand the rules of the game

Organisational checklist

- Vote with your feet. Develop a list of organisations that have reputations for having a learning culture, that value diversity in the workforce and in thinking, and are tackling factors such as unconscious bias and stereotyping. Ask other women. Women will self-select in and out of organisations based on this intelligence.

- Head to where there are women in executive and senior positions. Evidence shows that the strongest predictor of women's progress to senior executive roles is the number of women working in that area. Look not only at numbers of women in senior positions, but also where these women are located. Are they in business-facing, operational roles with profit-and-loss responsibilities that could be the pipeline to senior roles?

- Look at the style of women in senior roles as an indicator of what the CEO values.

A Checklist for Successful Career Navigation

- Undertake company research. Read recent speeches by the head of HR, the CFO and the CEO. What the key leaders give airtime to is what they truly value.

- Investigate the culture of the organisation from as many perspectives as possible — inside the organisation, former employees, customers and possibly the investment community. Probe the culture deeply around:

  - The type of people who get promoted

  - What is valued, which would lead to someone being considered for a promotion

  - How the big issues are managed (ideally, cite a recent acquisition or major change)

  - How failures are handled

  - How the organisation is perceived around achieving diversity at senior levels

  - How disagreements with the CEO are handled

  - How the organisation deals with challenges to current thinking or disagreement

  - Other people's career experiences in this organisation.

The leader/CEO

- What gets measured and rewarded, including targets for diversity?

- Are women being given opportunities to lead challenging strategic projects?

- Evidence of diversity in the team

- How decisions are made — empowerment and control

- Reputation of the manager among other women

- Track record of championing women

Leader/CEO checklist

- Look at the CEO's focus. Any CEO who is serious about the issue will set targets and hold managers accountable — not just on numbers of women but on implementation of broader diversity initiatives that are accessed by the whole workforce, like flexible work practices and part-time work. These actions set the culture.

- Find out what are the top, most exciting value-creation opportunities being pursued by the organisation and how many women are working on them.

- Look for diversity in the team reporting to the leader. Is he or she appointing team members with diverse backgrounds, opinions and perspectives, or just like-minded people?

Action Plan

The Action Plan and checklists in the pages that follow provide a structure to help you plan your career, based on the three-stage model described above. While this model emphasises women's careers, diverse cultures are indicative of learning cultures and so this Action Plan will have enormous benefits to any individual seeking an organisation where they can learn, grow and realise their potential.

Personal Checklist

Priority	What I need to do	Who I need to speak to
Understand my personal mission and values		
Understand my passions		
Describe what exciting and challenging work means to me		
Document my achievements		
Be clear about my ideal role — what I must have and will not compromise on, would like to have, and must avoid		
Have a current resume		
Develop my internal networks		
Develop my external networks		
Develop a list of networking organisations I may be interested in joining		
Other activities		

Action Plan

By when	Outcome and next steps

Organisational Checklist

Priority	What I need to do	Who I need to speak to
Develop a list of organisations with a track record in supporting women		
Research speeches or presentations made by key decision-makers in identified organisations		
Research the organisation's policies and practices around diversity		
Keep a scrapbook of relevant news articles.		
Identify from my networks a number of individuals in my target organisations whom I can interview		
Prepare questions for each networking interview		
Other activities		

Action Plan

By when	Outcome and next steps

Leader/CEO Checklist

Priority	What I need to do	Who I need to speak to
Identify KPIs that the CEO measures and manages		
Identify key strategic projects and who is working on them		
Assess diversity of the top team and the business unit or area in which I have an interest		
Identify where women are located in the organisation and how they got there		
Gather intelligence on the reputation of the CEO or leader, his/her career path and achievements		
Understand the leader's personal leadership style, decision-making processes and what he/she values		
Other activities		

Action Plan

By when	Outcome and next steps

Notes

NORAH BREEKVELDT

1 R. E. Steinpreis, K. A. Anders and
   D. Ritzke, *The Impact of Gender on
   the Review of the Curricula Vitae of
   Job Applicants and Tenure Candidates:
   A National Empirical Study*, University
   of Wisconsin-Milwaukee, 1999,
   http://advance.cornell.edu/documents/
   ImpactofGender.pdf.

2 J. Correll, S. Benard and I. Paik, 'Getting
   A Job: Is There a Motherhood Penalty?',
   American Journal of Sociology (No. 112,
   2007, pp. 1297–1338).

3 C. Good, J. Aronson and J. A. Harder,
   'Problems in the Pipeline: Stereotype
   Threat and Women's Achievement in
   High-level Maths Courses', *Journal of
   Applied Development Psychology* (Vol. 29,
   No. 1, 2008, pp. 17–28).

4 Zenger Folkman, *A Study in Leadership:
   Women Do It Better than Men*, 2012,
   http://www.zfco.com/media/articles/ZFCo.
   WP.WomenBetterThanMen.033012.pdf.

5 Accenture, *The High-Performance
   Workforce Study 2010*, http://www.
   accenture.com/SiteCollectionDocuments/
   PDF/Accenture_The_High_Performance_
   Workforce_Study_2010.pdf.

6 See, for instance, Chief Executive Women,
   *The Business Case for Women as Leaders:
   A CEW Discussion Paper*, February 2009.

DR HANNAH PITERMAN

1 Bronwyn Pike, 'Truth is, We Really
   Haven't Come a Long Way, Baby', *The Age*,
   20 October 2012.

2 Jacob Rosenberg, *The Hollow Tree* (Crows
   Nest, NSW: Allen & Unwin, 2008).

3 Bill George, Peter Sims and Andrew
   McLean, 'Discovering Your Authentic
   Leadership', *Harvard Business Review*
   (February 2007, pp. 129–138).

4 Office for Women, *Lifting and Raising
   the Bar* (Canberra: Commonwealth of
   Australia, 2006).

5 C. MacKinnon and R. Siegel, *Directions in
   Sexual Harassment Law* (New Haven, CT:
   Yale University Press, 2004), p. 170.

6 Equal Employment for Women in the
   Workplace Agency (EOWA), *Australian
   Census for Women in Leadership 2012*.

7 NATSEM, 'The Impact of a Sustained
   Gender Wage Gap on the Economy',
   Report to the Office for Women,
   Department of Families, Community
   Services, Housing and Indigenous Affairs.

8 Federal Government's Workplace Gender
   Equality Agency.

9 V. Sojo and R. Wood, 'Resilience: Women's
   Fit, Functioning and Growth at Work:
   Indicators and Predictors' (Centre for
   Ethical Leadership, Melbourne Business
   School, University of Melbourne, 2012).

10 Section 65 of the *Fair Work Act 2009*.

11 B. Pocock, 'The Regulation of Women's
    Employment in Australia: What Lessons
    for China?', Women's Labour Rights
    Workshop, Fuzhou, Fujian Province,
    20–23 November 2007.

12 H. Piterman, 'The Leadership Challenge:
    Women in Management', (Department
    of Families, Housing, Community
    Services and Indigenous Affairs, 2008);
    H. Piterman, *Unlocking Gender Potential:
    A Leader's Handbook* (Highett, Vic.: Major
    Street Publishing, 2010).

13 S. Orbach and L. Eichenbaum, *Between
    Women* (London: Random House, 1994).

14 Christopher Thomas, *Agender in the
    Boardroom*, North Sydney: EOWA and Egon
    Zehnder, 2008).

15 Goldman Sachs JB Were, 'Australia's
    Hidden Resource: The Economic Case for
    Increasing Female Participation', research
    report, 26 November 2009.

16 *Enterprising Nation: Renewing Australia's Managers to Meet the Challenges of the Asia-Pacific Century*, Report of the Industry Task Force on Leadership and Management Skills (Commonwealth of Australia, 1995).

17 Piterman, 'The Leadership Challenge' and *Unlocking Gender Potential*.

18 H. Piterman and L. Richie, 'Women in Leadership: Looking below the Surface' (Committee for Economic Development of Australia, 2010).

19 Catalyst, 'The Double-Bind Dilemma for Women in Leadership', 2007, http://www.catalyst.org/system/files/The_Double_Bind_Dilemma_for_Women_in_Leadership_Damned_if_You_Do_Doomed_if_You_Dont.pdf.

20 http://humanrights.gov.au/sex_discrimination/male-champions/index.html

21 E. Knight, 'Follow These Three Easy Steps to More Women in Boardrooms', *Business Day*, 13 October 2011.

22 Simone de Beauvoir, *The Second Sex*, trans. and ed. by H. M. Parshley (New York: Bantam, Knopf, 1952).

23 S. Reciniello, 'Is Woman the Future of Man?', *Organization & Social Dynamics* (Vol. 11, No. 2, 2011, pp. 151–174).

24 ibid, p. 160.

Dr Kerry Baxter

1 B. Russell, *History of Worker Philosophy* (New York: Routledge, 1995), p. 63.

2 The *complexity* concepts of *attractors* and *fractals* were used in the study as metaphorical constructs. The attractor metaphor is used in a thought-provoking way to identify the connections between the lived career experience (human interaction) of the professional women in the study and what motivated and guided their attitudes and behaviours in relation to their taking of executive positions in corporate organisations. According to L. Kuhn (*Adventures in Complexity: For Organisations near the Edge of Chaos* [Devon, UK: Triarchy Press, 2009], p. 15),

complexity concepts or metaphors can be used as tools for developing new insights and understandings of the organisational forms, processes, practices, issues and problems highlighted through fractal fragments. The implications of fractality for this study are exciting. Through fractal narrative analysis, each woman's individual narrative can be examined for patterns or characteristics of similarity. See: L. Kuhn and R. Woog, 'From Complexity Concepts to Creative Applications', *World Futures: The Journal of General Evolution* (Vol. 63, Nos. 3–4, April–June 2007, pp. 176–193).

3 S. A. Hewlett, *Off-Ramps and On-Ramps: Keeping Talented Women on the Road to Success* (Boston: Harvard Business School Press, 2007).

4 Kuhn, *Adventures in Complexity*.

5 T. Porter-O'Grady and K. Malloch, *Quantum Leadership: Textbook for New Leadership* (Sudbury, MA: Jones and Bartlett Publishers, 2003), p. 37.

6 D. Merrill-Sands, J. Kickul and C. Ingols, 'Women Pursuing Leadership and Power: Challenging the Myth of the Opt-out Revolution', *CGO Insights* (Boston: Center for Gender in Organizations, Simmons School of Management, February 2005).

Ann Sherry, AO

1 Carnival Australia represents seven of the international cruise brands operating in the local market: P&O Cruises, P&O Cruises World Cruising, Cunard, Princess Cruises, Carnival Cruise Lines, Holland America Line, and Seabourn.

2 Ruth Pollard, 'Full Steam Ahead for Carnival CEO Ann Sherry', *Sydney Morning Herald*, 4 June 2011.

Sarah Rey & Mary-Jane Ierodiaconou

1 Virginia Harrison, 'Women Slide in Partnership Ranks', *The Australian*, 25 June 2010, http://www.theaustralian.com.au/business/legal-affairs/women-slide-in-partnership-ranks/story-e6frg97x-1225884034943.

THERESA GATTUNG

1   Helen Place, *Managing Your Brilliant Career: A Guide for Women in Management* (Auckland: Motivation Inc., 1982).

2   Theresa Gattung, *Bird on a Wire* (Auckland: Random House, 2009)

3   Chris Hunt, 'Banking Crises in New Zealand: An Historical Overview', paper prepared for the RBNZ/VUW Professorial Fellowship Workshop, Wellington, 17 June 2009, pp. 31–32 (available at http://www.rbnz.govt.nz/research/workshops).

4   *The Independent*, 10 April 2002.

5   *The Dominion-Post*, 15 July 2002.

6   'The World's Most Powerful Women', *Forbes* magazine, 8 September 2006.

7   'Boston Consulting Group Report', *New Zealand Herald*, 2 July 2008.

8   Gattung, *Bird on a Wire*, p. 248.

TERRI JANKE

1   *Milpurrurru v Indofurn Pty Ltd*, 1995: an Australian company copied and adapted various Indigenous works of art, and had them woven into carpets in Vietnam and imported into Australia. Permission to use the designs was never sought. An award of almost $200,000 was made to the eight artists involved, and the offending carpets were withdrawn from sale. By 1996, Indofurn had been wound up and the director declared bankrupt; the artists have not received a cent. See: T. Janke, 'Federal Court Awards Record Damages to Aboriginal Artists', *Queensland Community Arts Network News* (No. 1, 1998, p. 89).

2   T. Janke, *Butterfly Song* (Camberwell, Vic.: Penguin Group Australia, 2005).

NAOMI SIMSON

1   Liz Wiseman, *Multipliers: How the Best Leaders Make Everyone Smarter* (New York: HarperCollins, 2010)

FARAH FAROUQUE

1   Louise North, 'Bloke Newsroom Culture', *Media International Australia* (No. 132, 2009, pp. 5–15).

2   The Social Studio: http://www.thesocialstudio.org/faq/The_Social_Studio_FAQ/FAQ_FAQ.html.

ANNWYN GODWIN

1   Australian Public Service (APS), 'Flexibility and Gender Equality Journey', PowerPoint presentation, working draft, 21 September 2012.

2   *Australian Census of Women in Leadership 2012*, p. 1

CATHERINE NANCE

1   H. Rosin, *The End of Man and the Rise of Women* (New York: Riverhead, 2012).

2   Australian Bureau of Statistics (ABS), 'Table 03. Labour Force Status by Sex', *Labour Force, Australia, October 2012*, Catalogue No. 6202.0.

3   ABS, *Year Book Australia, 2012*, Catalogue No. 1301.0.

4   ABS, *Australian Social Trends, 1994*, Catalogue No. 4102.0.

5   ABS, *Australian Social Trends, September 2012*, Catalogue No. 4102.0.

6   ibid.

7   R. Layne, Marketing Summit, researchhub.com.au, 2008.

8   ABS, *Deaths, Australia, 2011*, Catalogue No. 3302.0.

9   *Australian Census of Women in Leadership 2012*.

10 *Wire*, 'Media Release: Subtle Workplace Discrimination Holding Women Back (29/9/11)', www.wire.org.au/media-release.

11 'Board of Directors in Australia, 1994', Australian Institute of Company Directors and Korn/Ferry International survey of 188 organisations.

12 J. McCann and J. Wilson, *Background Note: Representation of Women in Australian Parliaments*, Parliamentary Library, 7 March 2012.

13 Australian Public Service Commission, *Statistical Bulletin 2010/2011*, http://www.apsc.gov.au/stateoftheservice/1011/statsbulletin/index.html, accessed 4 April 2012.

14 Department of Families, Housing, Community Services and Indigenous Affairs, 'Women on Australian Government Boards Report 2009–2010', http://www.fahcsia.gov.au/sa/women/pubs/govtint/Pages/women_aus_govt_board_rpt_2010.aspx.

15 World Economic Forum, *The Global Gender Gap Report 2011*, http://reports.weforum.org/global-gender-gap-2011.

16 ibid.

17 ABS statistics from the 'Experience Works' report, July 2009, in *Employment and Retention Strategies of Older Workers*, Roundtable Discussion Paper, Office of Ageing, June 2010, p. 6.

18 ibid, p. 6.

19 ibid, p. 4.

20 *Females in the Labour Force*, IBISWorld Business Environment Report, October 2012.

21 *Increasing Participation among Older Workers: The Grey Army Advances*, Deloitte Access Economics, 2012, p. ii.

22 L. Liswood, *The Loudest Duck: Moving Beyond Diversity While Embracing Differences to Achieve Success at Work* (Hoboken, NJ: John Wiley & Sons, 2010).

23 S. Van Yoder, *Coping with the Ageing Workforce* (2002), cited in Bradley Jorgensen, Hudson (Global Resources & Human Capital Solutions), *The Ageing Population: Implications for the Australian Workforce*, August 2004, p. 9.

24 R. M. Merril, S. G. Aldana, J. E. Pope, D. R. Anderson, C. R. Coberley and R. W. Whitmer, and HERO Research Study Subcommittee, *Presenteeism according to Health Behaviours, Physical Health and Work Environment*, http://www.the-hero.org/Research/Stdies.htm.

25 B. F. Jones, *Age and Great Invention*, National Bureau of Economic Research, Working Paper No. 11359.

26 'The Golden Age of Innovation', *Newsweek*, 20 August 2010.

27 'A Business Case for Women', *McKinsey Quarterly*, September 2008, p.1.

28 *Increasing Participation among Older Workers*.

29 Goldman Sachs JB Were, *Australia's Hidden Resource: The Economic Case For Increasing Female Participation*, 2009.

30 *Income, Superannuation and Debt Pre- and Post-retirement*, AMP.NATSEM Income and Wealth Report, Issue 7, March 2004, p. 2.

31 ibid.

32 ABS statistics from 'Experience Works', p. 4.

33 Liswood, *The Loudest Duck*, p. 49.

34 L. Rudman et al., *Status Incongruity and Backlash Effects: Defending the Gender Hierarchy Motivates Prejudice toward Female Leaders*, cited in C. Fine, *Delusions of Gender* (London: Icon Books, 2010), p. 59.

35 ibid, p. 58.

HEATHER CARMODY

1 The *Equal Employment Opportunity (EEO) for Women Act* was introduced in Australia in 1975, and the *Sex Discrimination Act* was passed in 1984.

2 'Key Statistics — Australian Small Business' (Department of Innovation, Industry, Science and Research, Commonwealth of Australia, 2011), p. 3.

3 Reported in D. Jacobs, 'How to Survive the Turnover Tidal Wave', *Business Spectator*, 20 June 2012.

4 Myriam Robbin, 'What Can You Get Done in Four Years?', *Leading Company*, 11 April 2012, http://www.leadingcompany.com.au/new-research/what-can-you-get-done-in-four-years/20120411611.

5 H. Rosin, *The End of Men and the Rise of Women* (New York: Penguin, 2012).

KATHERINE TEH-WHITE

1 M. Csikszentmihalyi, *Flow: The Psychology of Optimal Experience* (New York: Harper and Row, 1990).

HUGH DAVIES

1 Hugh Davies, *The Titanium Professional* (Melbourne: Business and Professional Publishing, 2000). The table of values and practices can be found on pages 178–179. The first four of these draw directly from Daniel Goleman's conception of emotional intelligence (*Emotional Intelligence* [London: Bloomsbury, 1996]). The last rests perhaps more on conventional definitions of IQ.

Additional Reading

Accenture, *Women Leaders and Resilience: Perspectives from the C-Suite International Women's Day 2010*, Global Research Results, March 2010

Australian Bureau of Statistics, *Labour Mobility*, February 2012, Catalogue No. 6209.0.

Barsh, J., Devillard, S. and Wan, J. 'The Global Gender Agenda', *McKinsey Quarterly*, November 2012.

Barsh, J. and Lee, L. *Unlocking the Full Potential of Women at Work*, McKinsey & Company.

Barta, T., Kleiner, M. and Neumann, T. 'Is There a Payoff from Top–Team Diversity?', *McKinsey Quarterly*, April 2012.

Catalyst, *The Bottom Line: Corporate Performance and Women's Representation on Boards (2004–2008)*, 2011.

Credit Suisse, *Gender Diversity and Corporate Performance*, 2012.

EOWA, *Australian Census of Women in Leadership 2012*, Australian Government, www.eowa.gov.au.

Fine, C. *Delusions of Gender: How Our Minds, Society and Neurosexism Create Difference*. New York: W. W. Norton & Co., 2012.

Fox, C. *7 Myths about Women and Work*. Sydney: NewSouth Publishing, 2012.

Goldman Sachs JB Were, *Australia's Hidden Resource: The Economic Case for Increasing Female Participation*, Research Report, 26 November 2009.

Liswood, L. *The Loudest Duck: Moving beyond Diversity while Embracing Differences to Achieve Success at Work*. New Jersey: John Wiley & Sons, 2010.

Male Champions of Change, Australian Human Rights Commission, *Our Experiences in Elevating the Representation of Women in Leadership: A Letter from Business Leaders*, 2011.

Additional Reading

McKinsey & Company, 'A Business Case for Women', *McKinsey Quarterly*, September 2008.

McKinsey & Company, *Moving Women to the Top: McKinsey Global Survey Results*, 2010.

McKinsey & Company, 'Women at the Top of Corporations: Making It Happen', *Women Matter* report, 2010.

Piterman, H. *The Leadership Challenge: Women in Management*. Hannah Piterman Consulting Group, published by the Department of Families, Housing, Community Services and Indigenous Affairs, March 2008.

Piterman, H. *Unlocking Gender Potential: A Leader's Handbook*. Highett, Vic.: Major Street Publishing, 2010.

Piterman, H. *Women in Leadership: Looking Below the Surface*, CEDA report, 2011.

Rayner, M. and Kirner, J. *The Women's Power Handbook*. Ringwood, Vic.: Viking, 1999.

Sandberg, S. *Lean in: Women, Work and the Will to Lead*. Toronto: Knopf Borzoi Books, Random House, 2013.

Sanders, M., Hrdlicka, J., Hellicar, M., Cottrell, D. and Knox, J. *What Stops Women from Reaching the Top?: Confronting the Tough Issues*. Bain & Company, Inc., 2011.

Sinclair, A. *Trials at the Top*. Melbourne: The Australian Centre, The University of Melbourne, 1994.

The 100% Project, *Men at Work: What They Want and Why It Matters for Women*, 2011.

Zenger Folkman, *A Study in Leadership: Women Do It Better than Men*, 2012, http://www.zfco.com/media/articles/ZFCo.WP.WomenBetterThanMen.033012.pdf.

Thank you for reading *Sideways To The Top*.

To engage in discussion, visit:
www.facebook.com/sideways-to-the-top

For professional advice about developing your career and moving sideways to the top, visit:
www.macfarlanlane.com.au

Follow us on Twitter at:
twitter.com/sidewaystotop